Report written by

Tom Cox

Amanda Griffiths

Eusebio Rial-González

Institute of Work, Health & Organisations
University of Nottingham Business School
Jubilee Campus, Wollaton Road
Nottingham NG8 1BB
United Kingdom

Contents

FOREWORD

Stress at work is a priority issue of the European Agency for Safety and Health at Work. As part of the Agency's 1999 programme, an information project was launched in order to collect, evaluate and review research data on work-related stress and its causes, and on intervention studies.

The Institute of Work, Health and Organisations at the University of Nottingham, United Kingdom, was appointed to carry out this project within the framework of the Topic Centre on Research – Work and Health. This report on "Research on Work-related Stress" has been prepared by Professor Tom Cox CBE, Dr. Amanda Griffiths and Mr. Eusebio Rial-González from that Institute.

A special consultation process was conducted in the autumn of 1999 by sending the draft manuscript to the members of the Thematic Network Group on Research - Work and Health, to the European Commission, to the European social partners and to other experts on the topic. The draft Report was also presented at a Joint Consensus Workshop organised by the National Institute of Occupational Health (Denmark) and the Institute of Work, Health and Organisations (United Kingdom) in Copenhagen on 25th–26th October 1999. Following the consultation process, the final report was prepared and published.

The European Agency wishes to thank the authors for their comprehensive work. The Agency wishes to thank also the participants in the Copenhagen workshop and all those individuals otherwise involved in the review process.

May 2000

European Agency for Safety and Health at Work

EXECUTIVE SUMMARY

The European Agency for Safety and Health at Work commissioned this Status Report on stress at work within the framework of the Topic Centre on Research – Work and Health (TC/WH). The Report considers early and contemporary scientific studies on the nature of stress at work, on its effects on health and on the way in which such knowledge is being applied in attempts to manage this problem. The Topic Centre on Good Practice – Stress at Work (TC/GP-ST) collects and evaluates good practice information on stress at work both within the EU and beyond. Consequently, this Report deals with the research evidence regarding the assessment and management of stress at work: it does not review stress management in practice. However, it discusses the conceptual frameworks implied in the practice of stress management at work and in current health and safety legislation, focusing in

particular on the utility of the 'control cycle' and problem-solving approaches to the management of stress at work.

Introduction

Over the past three decades, there has been a growing belief in all sectors of employment and in government that the experience of stress at work has undesirable consequences for the health and safety of individuals and for the health of their organisations. This belief has been reflected both in public and media interest and in increasing concern voiced by the trades unions, and professional and scientific bodies.

There are three basic questions that need to be answered:
(1) What is the nature of stress at work?
(2) Does work stress affect health and well-being and, if so, how? and
(3) What are the implications of existing research for the management of work-related stress?

This Report addresses these questions after having briefly examined the difficulties involved in placing work stress in the context of other life stressors.

The Extent of the Problem

Determining the extent of stress-related health problems at work is not an easy task. Most countries routinely collect data on ill-health retirements, work days lost due to sickness, injury and disability, etc. However, such data are imprecise and not reliable in terms of describing trends due to changes in, for example, the recording methods used. For this reason, they can only be used as a basis for 'educated guesses' in relation to the extent or cost of occupational stress. It is even more difficult to obtain valid, reliable and standardised data across the European Union's 15 Member States. As the 1997 European Foundation report on European Working Environment in Figures suggested, "although some information sources exist, very little comparable quantitative occupational health and safety data is available at European level, at present." (European Foundation, 1997).

The European Foundation's 1996 Working Conditions in the European Union revealed that 57% of the workers questioned believed that their work affected their health. The work-related health problems mentioned most frequently are musculoskeletal complaints (30%) and stress (28%). 23% of respondents said they had been absent from work for work-related health reasons during the previous 12 months. The average number of days' absence per worker was 4 days per year, which represents around 600 million working days lost per year across the EU.

Although there is obviously a need for more rigorous data collection mechanisms, it is clear that stress-related ill-health is a major cause for concern in terms of its impact on both individuals' lives and the productivity of organisations and countries. The research summarised in this Report shows that, even within a life perspective, work-related stress is a significant problem and represents a major challenge to occupational health in Europe.

Definition of Stress

The definition of stress is not simply a question of semantics –playing with words– and it is important that there is agreement, at least in broad terms, on its nature. A lack of such agreement would seriously hamper research into stress and the subsequent development of effective stress management strategies.

The simple equating of demand with stress has been associated with the belief that a certain amount of stress is linked to maximal performance and possibly good health. Belief in optimal levels of stress has been used, on occasions, to justify poor management practices. Given this, it is an unfortunate but popular misconception that there is little consensus on the definition of stress as a scientific concept or, worse, that stress is in some way undefinable and unmeasurable. This belief belies a lack of knowledge of the relevant scientific literature.

It has been concluded in several different reviews of the stress literature that there are essentially three different, but overlapping, approaches to the definition and study of stress. The first approach conceptualises occupational stress as an aversive or noxious characteristic of the work environment, and, in related studies, treats it as an independent variable – the environmental cause of ill health. This has been termed the 'engineering approach'. The second approach, on the other hand, defines stress in terms of the common physiological effects of a wide range of aversive or noxious stimuli. It treats stress as a dependent variable – as a particular physiological response to a threatening or damaging environment. This has been termed the 'physiological approach'. The third approach conceptualises work stress in terms of the dynamic interaction between the person and their work environment. This final approach has been termed the 'psychological approach'.

Two specific criticisms have been offered of the first two approaches: the first empirical and the second conceptual. First, both engineering and physiological models do not adequately account for the existing data. For instance, they ignore the mediation of strong cognitive as well as situational (context) factors in the overall stress process. The second criticism is that the engineering and physiological models of stress are conceptually dated in that they are set within a relatively simple stimulus-response paradigm, and largely ignore individual differences of a psychological nature and the perceptual and cognitive processes that might underpin.

These two approaches, therefore, treat the person as a passive vehicle for translating the stimulus characteristics of the environment into psychological and physiological response parameters. They largely ignore the interactions between the person and their various environments, which are an essential part of systems-based approaches to biology, behaviour and psychology. However, the third approach to the definition and study of stress pays special attention to environmental factors and, in particular, to the psychosocial and organisational contexts to work stress. Stress is either inferred from the existence of problematic person-environment interactions

or measured in terms of the cognitive processes and emotional reactions which underpin those interactions. This has been termed the 'psychological approach'.

The development of psychological models has been, to some extent, an attempt to overcome the criticisms levelled at the earlier approaches. There is now a consensus developing around this approach to the definition of stress. For example, psychological approaches to the definition of stress are largely consistent with the International Labour Organization's definition of psychosocial hazards (International Labour Organization, 1986: see later) and with the definition of well-being recommended by the World Health Organization (1986)[1]. They are also consistent with the developing literature on personal risk assessment (see, for example, Cox & Cox, 1993; Cox, 1993; Cox & Griffiths, 1994, 1996). These consistencies and overlaps suggest an increasing coherence in current thinking within occupational health and safety.

Variants of this psychological approach dominate contemporary stress theory, and among them two distinct types can be identified: the interactional and the transactional. The former focus on the structural features of the person's interaction with their work environment, while the latter are more concerned with the psychological mechanisms underpinning that interac-

---

[1] Well-being is a dynamic state of mind characterised by reasonable harmony between a person's abilities, needs, and expectations, and environmental demands and opportunities (World Health Organization, 1986). The individual's subjective assessment is the only valid measure of well-being available (Levi, 1992).

tion. Transactional models are primarily concerned with cognitive appraisal and coping. In a sense they represent a development of the interactional models, and are largely consistent with them.

There is a growing consensus on the definition of stress as a negative psychological state with cognitive and emotional components, and on its effects on the health of both individual employees and their organisations. Furthermore, there are now theories of stress which can be used to relate the experience and effects of work stress to exposure to work hazards and to the harmful effects on health that such exposure might cause. Applying such theories to the understanding of stress at work allows an approach to the management of work stress through the application of the notion of the control cycle. Such an approach has proved effective elsewhere in health and safety. It offers a systematic problem-solving system for continuous improvement in relation to work stress. There are several distinct areas in which more research is required: some relate to the individual, but others relate to the design and management of work and interventions to improve the work environment.

Individual Differences: work ability and coping

Coping is an important part of the overall stress process. However, it is perhaps the least well understood despite many years of research. It has been suggested that coping has three main features. First, it is a *process*: it is what the person actually thinks and does in a stressful encounter. Second, it is *context-dependent*: coping is influenced by the particular encounter or appraisal that initiates it and by the resources available to manage that encounter. Finally, coping as a process is and should be defined *'independent of outcome'*; that is, independently of whether it was successful or not. There have been two approaches to the study of coping: that which attempts to classify the different types of coping strategies and produce a comprehensive taxonomy, and that which considers coping as a problem-solving process.

Most contemporary theories of stress allow for individual differences in the experience of stress, and in how and how well it is coped with. Individual difference variables have been investigated as either: (1) components of the appraisal process, or (2) moderators of the stress-health relationship. Hence, researchers have asked, for example, to what extent are particular workers vulnerable to the experience of stress, or, for example, to what extent does, say, 'hardiness' moderate the relationship between job characteristics and worker health? This Report suggests that this distinction between individual differences as components of the appraisal process and moderators of the stress-outcome relationship can be easily understood in terms of transactional models of stress.

The experience of stress is partly dependent on the individual's ability to cope with the demands placed on them by their work, and on the way in which they subsequently cope with those demands, and relates issues of control and support. More information is required on the nature, structure and effectiveness of individuals' abilities to meet work demands and to cope with any subsequent stress. The need for more information on coping is widely recognised (see, for example, Dewe, 2000), but relatively less attention has been paid to the need better to understand the concept of work ability or competence, although this is being flagged in relation to ageing research (e.g., Griffiths, 1999a; Ilmarinen & Rantanen, 1999)

Methodological Issues

The available evidence supports a psychological approach to the definition of stress, and suggests that transactional models are among the most adequate and useful of those currently available. Within this framework, stress is defined as a psychological state which is both part of and reflects a wider process of interaction between the person and their (work) environment.

This process is based on a sequence of relationships between the objective work environment and the worker's perceptions, between those perceptions and the experience of stress, and between that experience, changes in behaviour and physiological function, and health. This sequence provides a basis for measurement, but the different measures which can be derived from the sequence cannot be easily or defensibly combined into a single stress index.

Logically the measurement of the stress state must be based primarily on self-report measures which focus on the appraisal process and on the emotional experience of stress. Measures relating to

appraisal need to consider the worker's perceptions of the demands on them, their ability to cope with those demands, their needs and the extent to which they are fulfilled by work, the control they have over work and the support they receive in relation to work. Therefore, eliciting and modelling the knowledge and perceptions of employees is central to the assessment and measurement process. Despite their obvious centrality and importance, self-report measures of appraisal and the emotional experience of stress are, on their own, insufficient. While their reliability can be established in terms of their internal structure or performance over time without reference to other data, their validity cannot.

The validity of self-report data has been questioned in particular with regard to the issue of "negative affectivity" (NA), which can be defined as "a general personality trait reflecting individual differences in negative emotionality and self-concept, i.e., concentrating on negative aspects of everything and experiencing considerable distress in all situations" (Watson & Clarke, 1984). NA would affect not only workers' perception of their work environment, but also their appraisal of their own psychological health status or well-being, thus becoming a confounding variable that could account for a large proportion of the correlations between perceived hazards and perceived outcomes.

The research literature is still divided on the extent to which NA or common method variance distort the assessment of the stress-strain relationship. However, there are ways in which the design of assessment instruments and procedures can contribute to ensuring that the data obtained are of good quality. It is clear that an assessment relying solely on appraisal would represent very weak evidence, and would need to be supported by data from other domains.

Triangulation of evidence overcomes the potential problems of NA to some extent. The principle of triangulation holds that, to be secure, a potential psychosocial or organisational hazard must be identified by cross-reference to at least three different types of evidence. The degree of agreement between those different points of view provides some indication of the reliability of the data and, depending on the measures used, their concurrent validity.

Applying this principle would require data to be collected from at least three different domains. This can be achieved by considering evidence relating to:

1. the objective and subjective antecedents of the person's experience of stress,
2. their self-report of stress, and
3. any changes in their behaviour, physiology or health status (which might be correlated with [1] and/or [2]).

The influence of moderating factors, such as individual and group differences may also be assessed. Confidence on the validity of the data thus obtained is supported by various studies which have shown that there is good convergence between self-report and supervisor- and subordinate-report. The use of any measure must be supported by data relating to its reliability

and validity, and its appropriateness and fairness in the situation in which it is being used. The provision of such data would conform to good practice in both occupational psychology and psychometrics (e.g., Cox & Ferguson, 1994), but may also be required if any subsequent decisions are challenged in law.

Work Hazards and Stress

In line with both the scientific literature and current legislation, this Report considers the evidence relating to all work hazards. These can be broadly divided into *physical hazards*, which include the biological, biomechanical, chemical and radiological, and the *psychosocial hazards*. Psychosocial hazards may be defined as "those aspects of work design and the organisation and management of work, and their social and environmental contexts, which have the potential for causing psychological, social or physical harm".

Exposure to physical and psychosocial hazards may affect psychological as well as physical health. The evidence suggests that such effects on health may be mediated by, at least, two processes: a direct physical mechanism, and a psychological stress-mediated mechanism. These two mechanisms do not offer alternative explanations of the hazard-health association; in most hazardous situations both operate and interact to varying extents and in various ways.

The psychological aspects of work have been the subject of research since at least the 1950s. Initially psychologists concentrated primarily on the obstacles to employees' adaptation and adjustment to the work environment, rather than on the potentially hazardous characteristics the workplace itself may have for workers. However, with the emergence of psychosocial work-environment research and occupational psychology in the 1960s, the focus of interest has moved away from an individual perspective and towards considering the impact of certain aspects of the work environment on health. There is now a large body of evidence that identifies a common set of work characteristics as potentially hazardous (see Table 1).

Additionally, large scale socio-economic and technological changes in recent years have affected workplaces considerably. They are often collectively referred to as "the changing world of work". This term encompasses a wide range of new patterns of work organisation at a variety of levels, such as:
- a growing number of older workers
- teleworking and increased use of information and communication technology (ICT) in the workplace
- downsizing, outsourcing, subcontracting and globalisation, with the associated change in employment patterns
- demands for workers' flexibility both in terms of number and function or skills
- an increasing proportion of the population working in the service sector
- self-regulated work and teamwork

The research corpus is still developing in these areas (e.g., see Rosenstock, 1997), but there is some preliminary evidence that even changes which may be thought to *enhance* the work environment can produce the opposite effect. For example,

Windel (1996) studied the introduction of self-regulating team work in the office of an electronics manufacturer. Although self-regulated work may be a source of increased self-efficacy and offer enhanced social support, Windel found that after 1 year work demands had increased and well-being decreased when compared to baseline data. The data suggested that the increase in social support brought about by self-regulating teams was not sufficient to counteract increased demands caused by the combination of a reduction in the number of staff and increases in managerial duties. Meta-analytical studies have also shown either mixed consequences (Bettenhausen, 1991; Windel & Zimolong, 1997) or higher rates of absenteeism and staff turnover (Cohen and Ledford, 1994) as a result of the implementation of team work or self-regulated work. It is clear that changes which have such a profound impact on the way organisations operate may carry associated potential hazards that need to be monitored for their impact on health and well-being.

In summary, it is possible from the available literature to explore the effects of the more tangible hazards of work on the experience of stress and on health, and to identify those psychosocial hazards which pose a threat to employees. Most literature reviews have identified the need for further research and development to translate this information into a form which can be used in the auditing and analysis of workplaces and organisations. Such a model, together with practical implementation strategies, has been provided by Cox *et al.* (2000).

Work and Health

Over the past two decades, there has been an increasing belief that the experience of stress necessarily has undesirable consequences for health. It has become a common assumption, if not a "cultural truism", that it is associated with the impairment of health. Despite this, the evidence is that the experience of stress does not *necessarily* have pathological sequelae. Many of the person's responses to that experience, both psychological and physiological, are comfortably within the body's normal homeostatic limits and, while taxing the psychophysiological mechanisms involved, need not cause any lasting disturbance or damage.

However, it is also obvious that the negative emotional experiences which are associated with the experience of stress detract both from the general quality of life and from the person's sense of well-being. Thus the experience of stress, while necessarily reducing that sense of well-being, does not inevitably contribute to the development of physical or psychological disorder. For some, however, the experience may influence pathogenesis: stress may affect health. At the same time, however, a state of ill health can both act as a significant source of stress, and may also sensitise the person to other sources of stress by reducing their ability to cope. Within these limits, the common assumption of a relationship between the experience of stress and poor health appears justified.

The Report presents a brief overview of the broad range of health and health-related effects which have been variously associated with the experience of stress. It focuses on changes in health and health-related behaviours and physiological function, which together may account for any linkage between that experience and psychological and physical health. In summary, the experience of stress can alter the way the person feels, thinks and behaves, and can also produce changes in their physiological function. Many of these changes simply represent, in themselves, a modest dysfunction and possibly some associated discomfort. Many are easily reversible although still damaging to the quality of life at the time.

However, for some workers and under some circumstances, they might translate into poor performance at work, into other psychological and social problems and into poor physical health. Nevertheless, the overall strength of the relationship between the experience of stress, and its antecedents, on one hand, and health, on the other, is consistent but moderate. There is evidence that the experience of stress at work is associated with changes in behaviour and physiological function, both of which may be detrimental to employees' health. Much is known about the possible mechanisms underpinning such effects, and particular attention has been paid to pathologies possibly associated with impaired immune activity as well as those more traditionally linked to stress, such as ulcers, coronary heart disease and rheumatoid arthritis.

Research into the Assessment and Management of Work-related Stress

There are numerous reviews of research into psychosocial hazards and stress and a large number of papers dealing with the stressors in almost every conceivable work setting and occupation. However, research into the nature and effects of a hazard is not the same as assessment of the associated risk. Indeed, most published studies would provide very little data that could be used for a risk assessment. Many "stress surveys" tend to identify only hazards or only outcomes, whereas the object of a risk assessment is to establish an *association* between hazards and health outcomes, and to evaluate the risk to health from exposure to a hazard.

An almost unavoidable corollary of the paucity of adequate risk assessments is that most "stress management" interventions target the individual rather than the organisation (the former is usually seen as cheaper and less cumbersome), are often *off-the-shelf* designs, and are entirely divorced from the process of diagnosis of the problems - if diagnosis takes place at all.

A different type of approach is therefore required in order to carry out risk assessments which can then inform the design of interventions - in other words, a strategy that actually *asks the question* before giving the answer. Such a strategy has already been suggested for the management of physical hazards at both EU and national level: the *control cycle*, which has been defined as "the systematic process by which hazards are identified, risks analysed and managed, and workers protected". As a systematic and comprehensive approach to assessing the risks within the work environment, the control cycle satisfies current legal requirements. However, it is still nec-

essary to evaluate whether it represents a scientifically valid and reliable strategy to assess psychosocial hazards. The Report examines the advantages and disadvantages of application of the control cycle (borrowed from the field of physical hazard control) to the assessment and management of work-related stress. The Report concludes that this model is very helpful as an analogy and represents a useful strategy for the assessment of psychosocial hazards at work. However, there are a number of issues to bear in mind:

a. the operationalisation of definitions of hazard,

b. the identification of adequate indices of harm that can also be reliably monitored,

c. satisfactory proof of a causal relationship, and

d. problems of measurement of the work environment.

Limitations of Contemporary Research into the Management of Work-related Stress

A review of the scientific literature suggests that there are a number of problems with research into the management of work-related stress.

1. Too narrow a view has often been taken of what constitutes stress management and there has been too strong a focus on 'caring for or curing' the *individual*.

2. Much of what has been offered, even in this narrow respect, either has a weak theoretical base or has been developed from theory outside occupational stress research.

3. There has been a tendency to treat the application of stress management strategies as a self-contained action and to divorce that application from any preceding process of problem diagnosis.

4. Stress management strategies often focus on single types of intervention and rarely are multiple strategies offered.

5. Such interventions are seldom offered for evaluation beyond participants' immediate reactions or measures of face validity.

There are three common purposes for evaluations of stress management programmes. The first is to ask whether the programme is effective; specifically whether the programme objectives are being met. A second purpose is to determine the efficiency or comparative effectiveness of two or more programmes or methods within a programme. The third purpose is to assess the cost-benefit or the cost-effectiveness of the programme.

Evaluation data on stress management programmes are relatively rare. There are relatively fewer cost-benefit and cost-effectiveness studies compared to studies on the overall effectiveness of programmes or the relative effectiveness of their component parts. What there is suggests that stress management programmes may be effective in improving the quality of working life of workers and their immediate psychological health, albeit self-reported. The evidence relating such interventions to improvements in physical health is weaker, largely for methodological reasons. There have been several authoritative reviews of organisational and personal stress management programmes in the last ten years reaching broadly similar conclusions.

It must be concluded that "the jury is still out" on stress management training: whilst it seems logical that such interventions should promote employee health, there are not yet sufficient data to be confident that they do. The evidence for employee assistance programmes, particularly those broadly conceived to include health promotion in the workplace, may be more encouraging, although that which relates to counselling alone is weak. The provision of counselling is largely designed to assist employees who are already suffering a problem, and is, in that sense, post hoc.

Stressor reduction / hazard control is, for several reasons, the most promising area for interventions, although again, there is not yet sufficient information to be confident about the nature and extent of their effectiveness. To date, such conclusions are based more on moral and strategic reasoning than on empirical data, although the data that do exist are supportive. What can be firmly concluded, however, is that there is still a need for further and more adequate evaluation studies.

Unfortunately, there are very few well designed and evaluated such interventions available in the literature to date. Nonetheless, Murphy et al. (1992) conclude that "job redesign and organisational change remain the preferred approaches to stress management because they focus on reducing or eliminating the sources of the problem in the work environment". However, they also point out that such approaches require a detailed audit of work stressors and a knowledge of the dynamics of organisational change if unwelcome outcomes are to be minimised. Further, such interventions can be expensive and more difficult and disruptive to design, implement and evaluate – factors which may make them less popular alternatives to secondary (reaction) and tertiary (treatment) interventions.

Nonetheless, Landy (1992) has summarised a number of possible interventions focused on the design of the work environment, and Murphy (1988) noted that, given the varieties of work stressors that have been identified, many other types of action relating to organisational and work development should be effective in reducing work stress. Van der Hek & Plomp (1997) also concluded that "there is some evidence that organization-wide approaches show the best results on individual, individual-organizational interface and organizational parameters [outcome measures]; these comprehensive programmes have a strong impact on the entire organization, and require the full support of management".

The emerging evidence is strong enough for the United States' National Institute for Occupational Safety and Health (NIOSH) to have identified "the organization of work" as one of the national occupational safety and health priority areas (Rosenstock, 1997). As part of their National Occupational Research Agenda (NORA), NIOSH intend to focus research on issues such as the impact of work organisation on overall health, the identification of healthy organisation characteristics and the development of intervention strategies.

The evaluation literature is inconclusive as to what are the exact mechanisms by which interventions, and particularly those focused on the individual, might affect health. Often, where different types of individually focused interventions have been compared, there is no evidence that any one or any combination is better than any other. This indicates that there may be a general, non-specific effect of intervening: the fact of an intervention may be beneficial, rather than its exact content. Interviews with managers responsible for introducing such interventions suggest that they are aware of such effects (see, for example, Cox et al., 1988). It is therefore possible that at least part of the effects of stress management programmes is due to the way they alter workers' perceptions of, and attitudes to, their organisations, and hence organisational culture. It was argued earlier that poor organisational culture might be associated with an increased experience of stress, while a good organisational culture might weaken or "buffer" the effects of stress on health. A defining factor for organisational culture is the size of the enterprise, and this should be borne in mind when considering intervention and evaluation issues, together with the wider context in terms of the socio-economic environment in the Member States.

Overall, the evidence on the effectiveness of stress management interventions reviewed in this Status Report is promising. The available data, although sparse, suggest that interventions, especially at the organisational level (e.g., Ganster et al., 1982; Shinn et al., 1984; Dollard & Winefield, 1996; Kompier et al., 1998), are beneficial to both individual and organisational health and should be investigated – and evaluated – further.

In summary, there is available scientific evidence to support the following:
• work-related stress is a current and future health and safety issue;
• work-related stress can be dealt with in the same logical and systematic way as other health and safety issues;
• the management of stress at work could be based on the adaptation and application of a control cycle approach such as that made explicit in contemporary models of risk management;
• there are already practical examples of this approach in several countries of the European Union.

The final comment concerns the maturity of stress research as an area of applied science. Two things must be apparent to the informed reader of this Report. First, there is a wealth of scientific data on work stress, its causes and effects, and on some of the mechanisms underpinning the relationships among these. More general research is not needed. What is required is an answer to the outstanding methodological questions, and to more specific questions about particular aspects of the overall stress process and its underpinning mechanisms. Second, although this wealth of scientific data exists, it still needs to be translated into practice, and the effectiveness of this practice evaluated. This is another set of needs, and one that will only be settled outside the laboratory and through the development of consensus and eventually common practice.

While stress at work will remain a major challenge to occupational health, our ability to understand and manage that challenge is improving. The future looks bright.

1.

TERMS OF REFERENCE

As part of its 1999 Work Programme, the European Agency for Safety and Health at Work commissioned this Report within the framework of the Topic Centre on Research – Work and Health (TC/WH) (see Appendix 1). Work-related stress is treated as an occupational health issue and current thinking and legislation in health and safety are used to frame this Report. Its prime objective is to provide an up-to-date overview of the scientific literature relating to research into the nature and effects of work-related stress and of stress management interventions.

It is not possible, within the terms of reference of this Report, to cite and appraise all the published literature because of both its vastness and its increasing specificity and detail (see for example, Danna & Griffin, 1999; Cartwright & Cooper, 1996; Cox, 1993; Borg, 1990; Hiebert & Farber, 1984; Kasl, 1990). Kasl (1992) has suggested that many reviews in this area are an attempt either to "paint the big picture" or to present a detailed evaluation of a specific hypothesis. The former can suffer because they are too superficial or too selective in favour of one over-arching view, while the latter can suffer simply because they fail to place the hypotheses of concern in their wider context and, thus, fail to make an evaluation on the basis of the whole picture. Furthermore, much of what is available for review has been deemed to be *methodologically weak*. For Kasl (1992), the main methodological problem is that the available evidence is, in large part, based on cross-sectional studies in which the key variables are measured and linked only in terms of self-report. While it would be unwise to reject out-of-hand all such studies, the methodological sophistication necessary for their proper design, analysis and interpretation is often also lacking. A second problem is that much of what is published is *redundant* in that it simply demonstrates well-established theories and would-be facts (Cox, 1993). In many cases there is no significant gain in knowledge.

There are also some important topics that cannot be explored in detail because of space constraints. For example, socio-economic and cultural factors –such as inequalities in health and health provision, particularly in relation to ageing and socio-economic status, new working patterns and the "global economy", cultural differences in attitudes towards work and health, etc.– are known to have an impact on work-related stress. Stress is also related to burnout, poor occupational safety and the reporting of work-related upper limb disorders. Although these are significant issues that should be borne in mind when considering the causes and consequences of stress at work, this Report can only deal with them briefly or indirectly in the space available (for instance, see sections 5.1, 5.2.1 and 5.4). Readers are therefore encouraged to consult other sources included in the Report's References section (e.g., European Agency, 1999).

Therefore, this Report focuses on that which is:
- relevant to its stated objective
- relevant to the treatment of work-related stress as an occupational health issue
- better known
- more, rather than less, adequate both methodologically and theoretically

By necessity, the Report also focuses primarily on the literature published in English. The authors acknowledge the impossibility of covering all the valuable research published in languages other than English within the constraints of time and resources. However, English has become the de facto lingua franca for scientific publication in Europe and, as a result, it is unlikely that this Report has missed any fundamental contributions.

This Report is, therefore, selective in the evidence that it draws on. At the same time, the Report is consistent with earlier guidance on the control and monitoring of psychosocial and organisational hazards prepared by the authors for the World Health Organization (European Region) and published in its Occasional Series in Occupational Health no. 5 (Cox & Cox, 1993), for the Health & Safety Executive of Great Britain (Cox, 1993; Cox et al., 2000), and for the Loss Prevention Council (UK) (Griffiths et al., 1998).

The European Agency's Topic Centre on Good Practice – Stress at Work (TC/GP-ST) collects, evaluates and disseminates existing good practice information about stress at work across the EU and beyond. Consequently, after reviewing the research into the nature, causes and effects of work-related stress, this Report deals briefly with the research evidence regarding the assessment and management of stress at work, but it does not examine actual stress management practice in detail.

2.

INTRODUCTION

Over the past three decades there has been a growing belief in all sectors of employment and in government that the experience of stress at work has undesirable consequences for the health and safety of individuals and for the health of their organisations. This belief has been reflected both in public and media interest and in increasing concern voiced by the trades unions, and professional and scientific bodies.

There are three basic questions that require answering:
1. What is the nature of occupational stress?
2. Does work stress affect health and well-being and, if so, how?
3. What are the implications of existing research for the management of work-related stress?

This Report addresses these questions after having briefly examined the difficulties involved in placing work stress in the context of other life stressors.

2.1

THE NATURE OF WORK-RELATED STRESS IN A LIFE PERSPECTIVE

There is evidence to suggest that work is only one of a number of possible areas or aspects of life that can give rise to the experience of stress and ill-health (e.g., Goldberg & Novack, 1992; Surtees & Wainwright, 1998). Largely following on from the work of Selye (1956), there has been an assumption that discrete, time-limited 'life events' requiring change or adaptation are associated with the experience of stress and may contribute to a wide range of disorders. Many attempts have been made to identify and scale such stressful life events (see, for example, Holmes & Rahe, 1967; Dohrenwend & Dohrenwend, 1974; Dohrenwend et al., 1988; Fisher, 1996). While psychometric research into the nature and impact of stressful life events is not without methodological problems (see, for example, Sarason et al., 1975; Perkins, 1988; Dohrenwend et al., 1988), some progress

has been made in determining the relative importance of different types of events. One particular example is considered here.

Dohrenwend et al. (1988) have described the careful development (and strengths and weaknesses) of the PERI[2] Life Events Scale. A list of 102 objectively verifiable life events was constructed from previous studies in New York. These events were classified according to 11 life domains: school, work, love and marriage, having children, family, residence, crime and legal matters, finances, social activities, health and miscellaneous. As in other studies (see Dohrenwend & Dohrenwend, 1974), subjects were asked to rate events against marriage, which was given an arbitrary rating of 500. Subjects were grouped according to a number of criteria such as age, sex, and ethnic background, and mean sub-group ratings were calculated for each event. This avoided giving undue weight to sub-groups over-represented in the overall sample. However, the events were also scored according to their mean rankings: this gave equal weight to all subjects regardless of sub group. Of the 102 life events, 21 related to work. The highest ranked work event was *suffered business loss or failure* with a mean rating of 510. *Demoted and promoted at work* rated 379 and 374 respectively. The lowest ranked work event was *changed job for one which was no better or worse than last one* (251). As far as non-work events were concerned, the highest ranked event overall was *child died* (with a rating of 1036), with *divorce* at 633, *married* at 500 (the

---

[2] PERI: Psychiatric Epidemiology Research Interview

anchor event) and the lowest, *acquired pet*, at 163. These data suggest that work-related life events are not trivial experiences, and are among those which have the greatest perceived impact. This conclusion is supported by a study in the United Kingdom which asked a sample of male and female employees in the East Midlands of England to identify that aspect (or domain) of their lives which presented them with the greatest problems and stress. Work was cited as the major source of problems and stress for 54% of respondents, while another 12% cited the work-home interface (Cox *et al.*, 1981).

However, it should be noted that where life event scales have included work events, the designers have been concerned only with discrete, 'acute' work-related events (such as being promoted or demoted). As will be argued in later sections of this Report, it is now widely thought that the primary stressors facing most employees in the course of their working life are chronic rather than acute and are rarely mentioned in life event scales. Some studies have also suggested that rankings of life events are context-dependent and can vary between different countries (Rahe, 1969) and between urban and rural communities (Abel *et al.*, 1987). Thus, although at first sight life event scales may seem to answer the question 'How important are work stressors?', in fact, they do not.

It is likely that there are interactions between stressors, both acute and chronic, which do not respect the boundary between work and non-work domains. Indeed, evidence does exist to suggest that work stress can 'spill over' to home life (Bacharach *et al.*, 1991; Burke, 1986), and vice versa (Quick *et al.*, 1992b), although effects may vary considerably (Kanter, 1977). The erroneous belief that work and non-work activities are unrelated in their psychological, physiological and health effects has been described as the 'myth of separate worlds' by Kanter (1977).

While it is nonsensical to attempt an exact determination of the relative importance of work and non-work stressors, because they are not independent in their effects, it is sensible to explore that interaction and the carry-over from one domain to the other. Although such interaction effects exist, they are not always obvious. When an acute stressful life event occurs in work or outside of work (such as the death of a loved one, or a serious injury), the initial impact of carry-over effects is often readily obvious to family, friends and colleagues or co-workers. However, when the effects of life stressors are more subtle and long lasting, carry-over effects are less frequently recognised and can be underestimated. Similarly, while the chronic experience of work stress may exert deleterious effects on family relationships, these may sometimes go undetected (see Gutek *et al.*, 1988; Repetti, 1987; Repetti & Crosby, 1984; Voydanoff & Kelly, 1984). A survey by the Canadian Mental Health Association (1984) found that 56% of respondents felt 'some' or 'a great deal of' interference between their jobs and home lives. Of particular concern were the 'amount of time that the job demanded' and the 'irregularity of working hours' (including shift work). The interference affected family routines and events, child rearing and household responsibilities, made employees moody at home and conflicted with leisure activities and social life.

The focus of this Report on work stress may suggest that work has only a negative effect on health: this is not the case. There is evidence that, under some circumstances, work may have positive health benefits, promoting psychological well-being (Baruch & Barnett, 1987) and physical health (Repetti et al., 1989). Unemployment and retirement from work are associated with excess risk of psychological ill health (for example, Lennon, 1999; Cobb & Kasl, 1977; Feather, 1990; Jackson & Warr, 1984; Kasl, 1980b; Warr, 1982, 1983, 1987). They may also be associated with increased risk of cardiovascular disease but the evidence here is, at best, equivocal (Kasl & Cobb, 1980). At the same time, specific work characteristics may also be beneficial to health, in particular, energy expenditure (Fletcher, 1988). Studies by Paffenbarger et al. (1977, 1984) have suggested that high-energy expenditure at work may be associated with reduced risks of fatal heart attacks.

The definition of work stress and its measurement are central to the question of its importance and the determination of carry-over effects – positive or negative. The following sections review both early and more contemporary theories of stress and explore their implications for measurement.

2.2

THE EXTENT OF
THE PROBLEM

Determining the extent of stress-related health problems at work is not an easy task. Most countries routinely collect data on ill-health retirements, work days lost due to sickness, injury and disability, etc. For example, between 1981-1994 the Netherlands recorded an increase from 21% to 30% in the percentage of workers who received a disability pension because of stress-related disorders (ICD-9, 309, adjustment disorder), and "the number who returned to work in the diagnosis group is lower than in any other group" (Van der Hek & Plomp, 1997).

However, such data are imprecise and not reliable in terms of describing trends due to changes in, for example, the recording methods used (see, Marmot & Madge, 1987; Fletcher, 1988; Jenkins, 1992, Griffiths, 1998). For this reason, they can only be used as a basis for 'educated guesses' in

relation to the extent or cost of occupational stress. It is even more difficult to obtain valid, reliable and standardised data across the European Union's 15 Member States. As the 1997 European Foundation report *European Working Environment in Figures* suggested, "although some information sources exist, very little comparable quantitative occupational health and safety data is available at European level, at present." (European Foundation, 1997)

The European Foundation's 1996 Working Conditions in the European Union revealed that 57% of the workers questioned believed that their work affected their health. The work-related health problems mentioned most frequently are musculoskeletal complaints (30%) and stress (28%). 23% of respondents said they had been absent from work for work-related health reasons during the previous 12 months. The average number of days' absence per worker was 4 days per year, which represents around 600 million working days lost per year across the EU.

Occupational diseases continue to give cause for concern across the European Union. Figure 1, for example, shows that –despite recent decreases– the number of occupational diseases reported in Germany grew dramatically during the 1990s and remains at a very high level (Bundesministerium für Arbeit und Sozialordnung, 1999).

To take the United Kingdom as another example, it has been suggested that upwards of 40 million working days are lost each year in the UK due to stress-related disorders (Kearns, 1986; Health & Safety

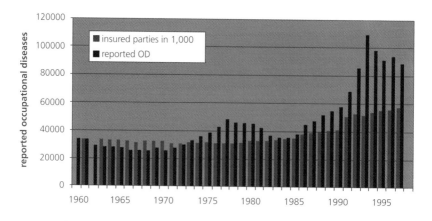

Reported occupational diseases in Germany 1960 to 1997
(source: Occupational Accident Prevention Report 1997)

Executive, 1990b; Jones et al., 1998). In 1994, the Health & Safety Executive of Great Britain published estimates (based on 1990 data) of the total cost to employers, the economy and society of work accidents and work-related ill health (Davies & Teasdale, 1994). The study attempted to quantify costs to all affected parties including employers (damage, lost output, costs of covering for sick absence), the medical services, the social security and insurance systems, as well as the costs to the victims of accidents and ill health, including "an amount to reflect the pain, grief and suffering involved". The study found that the cost of work accidents and work-related ill health to employers in the UK in 1990 was between £4.5 billion and £9 billion (6.84 – 13.7 billion euro approximately). Costs to victims and their families were about £4.5 billion. The total cost to the economy was between £6 billion and £12

billion (9.12 – 18.24 billion euro, about 1-2% of national output). Adding the sum for pain, grief and suffering yields a total cost to society of between £11 billion and £16 billion (16.72 – 24.32 billion euro). The framework can also be used to derive cost estimates for specific diseases (e.g. the Trades Union Congress (TUC) have estimated the cost of Repetitive Strain Injury to be £1 billion per year).

More recent figures released by the UK's Confederation of British Industry (1999) indicate that 200 million days were lost through sickness absence in 1998, an average of 8.5 days per employee. This represents a loss of 3.7% of working time. Absence from work cost British business £10.2 billion in 1998 (approximately 15.5 billion euro), an average cost of £426 per worker (approximately 647 euro). The survey shows that minor illness is the biggest cause of absence for manual and non-manual workers, with serious illness and home and family responsibilities also important for manual workers. For non-manual workers, workplace stress was felt to be the second highest contributor to absence, second only to minor illness.

The Health & Safety Executive of Great Britain has estimated that at least half of all lost days are related to work stress (Cooper et al., 1996). Furthermore, Kearns (1986) has suggested that up to 60% of all work absence is caused by stress-related disorders, while Cooper & Davidson (1982) have reported that 71% of their sample of managers in the United Kingdom felt that their psychological health problems were related to stress at work.

More adequate data exist on the relative architecture of stress-related ill health from general population surveys and from smaller scale studies of defined occupational populations (see, for example, Colligan et al., 1977; Eaton et al., 1990; Jones et al., 1998). In their questionnaire-based survey of the working population, Jones et al. (1998) found that 26.6% of the respondents reported suffering from work-related stress, depression or anxiety, or a physical condition which they ascribed to work-related stress. The authors estimated that 19.5 million working days[3] were lost in Great Britain due to work-related illness, of which 11 million were due to musculoskeletal disorders, and 5 million to stress. However, such figures must be treated with caution, since they rely mostly on uncorroborated self-report (Thomson et al., 1998). Other figures (such as the number of early retirements on the grounds of ill-health) which could help provide a general picture

in an *oblique* way have to be interpreted with similar caution (Griffiths, 1998).

From an international perspective, it has been estimated that approximately 550 million working days are lost each year in the US due to absenteeism (Harris *et al.*, 1985), of which 54% are thought to be stress-related (Elkin & Rosch, 1990). Projections from the National Health Interview Survey, suggested that 11 million workers in the United States could report 'health endangering' levels of stress at work (Shilling & Brackbill, 1987). Only loud noise was reported to be a more prevalent workplace hazard. Stress at work has become one of the main topics for the emergent discipline of occupational health psychology both in the United States (e.g., Quick *et al.*, 1997) and Europe.

In Australia, the Federal Assistant Minister for Industrial Relations estimated the cost of occupational stress to be around A$30 million[4] in 1994. The rising costs of work-related stress are illustrated by a recent study of 126 call centres (Deloitte & Touche, 1999), which revealed that impact of staff turnover and stress on call centre agents is costing organisations that use call centres to conduct business over the telephone a total of A$90 million a year. They found that stress-related absenteeism costs $150 per agent per year - a total cost of A$7.5 million per annum (approximately 4.54 million euro).

---

[3] Days lost per worker were defined as "number of days lost per person who has worked in the last 12 months, including people without a work-related illness".

[4] The Australian, June 17, 1994

2.3

SUMMARY

In a survey of the statutory bodies in all the EU Member States carried out by the European Agency for Safety and Health at Work, most of them identified stress and related psychosocial issues as a current and future priority (European Agency, 1998). Although there is a need for more rigorous data collection mechanisms, as identified by several bodies (e.g., European Foundation, 1997), it is clear that stress-related ill-health is a major cause for concern in terms of its impact on both individuals' lives and the productivity of organisations and countries. The research summarised in this section shows that, even within a life perspective, work-related stress is a significant problem and represents a major challenge to occupational health in Europe.

3.

DEFINING STRESS

The definition of stress is not simply a question of semantics –playing with words– and it is important that there is agreement, at least in broad terms, on its nature. A lack of such agreement would seriously hamper research into stress and the subsequent development of effective stress management strategies. Given this, it is an unfortunate but popular misconception that there is little consensus on the definition of stress as a scientific concept or, worse, that stress is in some way undefinable and unmeasurable. This belief belies a lack of knowledge of the relevant scientific literature.

3.1

CONCEPTUALISATION AND
FRAMEWORKS

It has been concluded in several different reviews of the scientific literature on stress that there are essentially three different, but overlapping, approaches to the definition and study of stress (Lazarus, 1966; Appley & Trumbull, 1967; Cox, 1978, 1990; Cox & Mackay, 1981; Fletcher, 1988, Cox, 1993). The first approach conceptualises occupational stress as an aversive or noxious characteristic of the work environment, and, in related studies, treats it as an independent variable –the environmental cause of ill health. This has been termed the 'engineering approach'. The second approach, on the other hand, defines stress in terms of the common physiological effects of a wide range of aversive or noxious stimuli. It treats stress as a dependent variable –as a particular physiological response to a threatening or damaging environment. This has been termed the 'physiological approach'. The

third approach conceptualises work stress in terms of the dynamic interaction between the person and their work environment. When studied, stress is either inferred from the existence of problematic person-environment interactions or measured in terms of the cognitive processes and emotional reactions which underpin those interactions. This final approach has been termed the 'psychological approach'. The engineering and physiological approaches are obvious among the earlier theories of stress, while the more psychological approaches characterise contemporary stress theory.

3.1.1 Engineering Approach

The engineering approach has treated stress as a *stimulus characteristic* of the person's environment, usually conceived in terms of the load or level of demand placed on the individual, or some aversive (threatening) or noxious element of that environment (Cox, 1978, 1990; Cox & Mackay, 1981; Fletcher, 1988). Occupational stress is treated as a property of the work environment, and usually as an objectively measurable aspect of that environment. In 1947, Symonds wrote, in relation to psychological disorders in the Royal Air Force flying personnel, that "stress is that which happens *to* the man, not that which happens *in* him; it is a set of *causes* not a set of *symptoms*." Somewhat later, Spielberger (1976) argued, in the same vein, that the term stress should refer to the objective characteristics of situations. According to this approach, stress was said to produce a strain reaction which although often reversible could, on occasions, prove to be irreversible and damaging (Cox & Mackay, 1981; Sutherland & Cooper, 1990). The concept of a stress threshold grew out of this way of thinking and individual differences in this threshold have been used to account for differences in stress resistance and vulnerability.

3.1.2 Physiological Approach

The physiological approach to the definition and study of stress received its initial impetus from the work of Selye (1950, 1956). He defined stress as "a state manifested by a specific syndrome which consists of all the non-specific changes within the biologic system" that occur when challenged by aversive or noxious stimuli. Stress is treated as a generalised and non-specific physiological response syndrome. For many years, the stress response was largely conceived of in terms of the activation of two neuroendocrine systems, the anterior pituitary-adrenal cortical system and the sympathetic-adrenal medullary system (Cox & Cox, 1985; Cox et al., 1983). The psychophysiology of stress is discussed in more detail in section 6.3.1. Selye (1950, 1956) argued that the physiological response was triphasic in nature involving an initial *alarm* stage (sympathetic-adrenal medullary activation) followed by a stage of *resistance* (adrenal cortical activation) giving way, under some circumstances, to a final stage of *exhaustion* (terminal reactivation of the sympathetic-adrenal medullary system). Repeated, intense or prolonged elicitation of this physiological response, it has been suggested, increases the wear and tear on the body, and contributes to what Selye (1956) has called the 'diseases of adaptation'. This apparently paradoxical term arises from the contrast between the immediate and short-term advantages bestowed by physiological response to stress (energy mobilisation for an active behavioural response) to the long-term disadvantages (increased risk of certain 'stress related' diseases).

Scheuch (1996) considers stress as one of the psychophysiological activities of human beings as they attempt to adapt to changes in the internal and external milieux. This activity relates to the quantity and quality of the relationship between demands and individual somatic, psychological and social capacities or resources in a specific material and social environment. Stress is understood by Scheuch as a reactive activity to a disturbed homeostatic state of organic functions, psychological functions and/or in the interaction between the human being and his or her social environment. The adaptation follows the principles of economisation of function, the principle of minimisation of effort, and the principle of well-being. Stress itself is the expression of a disorder of these principles (Scheuch, 1990, 1996).

Criticisms of Engineering & Physiological Approaches

Two specific criticisms have been offered of these two approaches: the first empirical and the second conceptual.

First, engineering and physiological models do not adequately account for the existing data. In relation to the engineering model,

consider the effects of noise on performance and comfort. The effects of noise
on task performance are not a simple function of its loudness or frequency but are
subject both to its nature and to individual
differences and context effects (see, for example, Cox, 1978; Flanagan et al. 1998;
Ahasan et al. 1999). Noise levels which are
normally disruptive may help maintain task
performance when subjects are tired or fa-
tigued (Broadbent, 1971), while even
higher levels of music may be freely chosen
in social and leisure situations.

Scott & Howard (1970) wrote: "certain
stimuli, by virtue of their unique meaning
to particular individuals, may prove problems only to them; other stimuli, by virtue
of their commonly shared meaning, are
likely to prove problems to a larger number
of persons." This statement implies the
mediation of strong cognitive as well as situational (context) factors in the overall
stress process (see below). This point has
been forcefully made by Douglas (1992)
with respect to the perception of risks (and
hazards). Such perceptions and related behaviours, she maintains, are not adequately explained by the natural science of
objective risk and are strongly determined
by group and cultural biases.

The simple equating of demand with stress
has been associated with the belief that a
certain amount of stress is linked to maximal performance (Welford, 1973) and possibly good health. Belief in optimal levels
of stress has been used, on occasions, to
justify poor management practices.

The physiological model is equally open to
criticism. Both the non-specificity and the

time course of the physiological response to
aversive and noxious stimuli have been
shown to be different from that described
by Selye (1950, 1956) and required by the
model (see Mason, 1968, 1971). Mason
(1971), for example, has shown that some
noxious physical stimuli do not produce the
stress response in its entirety. In particular,
he has cited the effects of heat. Furthermore, Lacey (1967) has argued that the low
correlations observed among different
physiological components of the stress response are not consistent with the notion of
an identifiable response syndrome. There is
also a difficulty in distinguishing between
those physiological changes which represent stress and those which do not, particularly as the former may be dissociated in
time from the stressor (Fisher, 1986).

There is now much research that suggests
that if the stress response syndrome exists
it is not non-specific. There are subtle but
important differences in the overall pattern
of response. There is evidence, for example, of differentiation in the response of
the catecholamines (reflecting sympathetic-adrenal medullary activation) to stressful
situations (Cox & Cox, 1985). Several dimensions have been suggested as a basis
of this differentiation but most relate to the
expenditure of effort of different types, for
example, physical versus psychological
(Dimsdale & Moss, 1980a, 1980b; S. Cox
et al., 1985). Dimsdale & Moss (1980b)
studied plasma catecholamine levels using
a non-obtrusive blood withdraw pump and
radioenzymatic assay. They examined 10
young physicians engaged in public speaking, and found that although levels of both
adrenaline and noradrenaline increased

under this set of demands, the levels of adrenaline were far more sensitive. This sensitivity was associated with feelings of emotional arousal which accompanied the public speaking. S. Cox and her colleagues (1985) examined the physiological response to three different types of task associated with short cycle repetitive work: urinary catecholamine excretion rates were measured using an adaptation of Diament & Byers (1975) assay technique. She found that both adrenaline and noradrenaline were sensitive to work characteristics, such as pay scheme and pacing, but differentially so. It was suggested that noradrenaline activation was related to the physical activity inherent in the various tasks, and to the constraints and frustrations present, while adrenaline activation was more related to feelings of effort and stress.

The second criticism is that the engineering and physiological models of stress are conceptually dated in that they are set within a relatively simple stimulus-response paradigm, and largely ignore individual differences of a psychological nature and the perceptual and cognitive processes that might underpin them (Cox, 1990; Sutherland & Cooper, 1990; Cox, 1993). These models treat the person as a passive vehicle for translating the stimulus characteristics of the environment into psychological and physiological response parameters. They also ignore the interactions between the person and their various environments which are an essential part of systems-based approaches to biology, behaviour and psychology. In particular, they ignore the psychosocial and organisational contexts to work stress.

3.1.3 Psychological Approach

The third approach to the definition and study of stress conceptualises it in terms of the dynamic interaction between the person and their work environment. When studied, it is either inferred from the existence of problematic person-environment interactions or measured in terms of the cognitive processes and emotional reactions which underpin those interactions. This has been termed the 'psychological approach'.

The development of psychological models has been, to some extent, an attempt to overcome the criticisms levelled at the earlier approaches. There is now a consensus developing around this approach to the definition of stress. For example, psychological approaches to the definition of stress are largely consistent with the International Labour Office's definition of psychosocial hazards (International Labour Organization, 1986) and with the definition of well-being recommended by the World Health Organization (1986)[5]. They are also consistent with the developing literature on personal risk assessment (see, for example, Cox & Cox, 1993; Cox, 1993; Cox & Griffiths, 1995, 1996). These consistencies and overlaps suggest an increasing coherence in current thinking within occupational health and safety.

Variants of this psychological approach dominate contemporary stress theory, and

---

[5] Well-being is a dynamic state of mind characterised by reasonable harmony between a person's abilities, needs, and expectations, and environmental demands and opportunities (WHO, 1986). The individual's subjective assessment is the only valid measure of well-being available (Levi, 1992).

–among them– two distinct types can be identified: the interactional and the transactional. The former focus on the structural features of the person's interaction with their work environment, while the latter are more concerned with the psychological mechanisms underpinning that interaction. Transactional models are primarily concerned with cognitive appraisal and coping. In a sense they represent a development of the interactional models, and are essentially consistent with them.

3.2

INTERACTIONAL THEORIES OF STRESS

Interactional theories of stress focus on the structural characteristics of the person's interaction with their work environment. Two particular interactional theories stand out as seminal among the various which have been offered: the Person-Environment Fit theory of French et al. (1982) and the Demand–Control theory of Karasek (1979). Neither is, however, without criticism: see, for example, Edwards & Cooper (1990) and Warr (1990).

3.2.1 Person-Environment Fit

Several researchers have suggested that the goodness of fit between the person and their (work) environment frequently offers a better explanation of behaviour than individual or situational differences (see, for example, Bowers, 1973; Ekehammer, 1974). Largely as a result of such observations, French and his colleagues formulated a the-

ory of work stress based on the explicit concept of the Person-Environment Fit (see, for example, French et al., 1982). Two basic aspects of fit were identified:

- The degree to which an employee's attitudes and abilities meet the demands of the job.
- The extent to which the job environment meets the workers' needs, and in particular the extent to which the individual is permitted and encouraged to use their knowledge and skills in the job setting.

It has been argued that stress is likely to occur, and well-being is likely to be affected, when there is a lack of fit in either or both respects (French et al., 1974). Two clear distinctions are made in this theory: first, between objective reality and subjective perceptions, and, second, between environmental variables (E) and person variables (P). Given this simple 2 x 2 configuration of P x E interaction, lack of fit can actually occur in four different ways, and each appear to challenge the worker's health. There can be both a lack of subjective and objective P-E fit: these are the main foci of attention with particular interest being expressed in the lack of subjective fit: how the worker sees their work situation. This provides a strong link with other psychological theories of stress. There can also be a lack of fit between the objective environment (reality) and the subjective environment (hence, lack of contact with reality), and also a lack of fit between the objective and subjective persons (hence, poor self-assessment).

French et al. (1982) have reported on a large survey of work stress and health in 23 different occupations in the United States and a sample of 2010 working men. The survey was framed by the P-E Fit theory, and, in their summary, the authors commented on a number of questions of theoretical and practical importance. In particular, they argued that their subjective measures mediated the effects of objective work on health. Their data showed that there was a good correspondence between the objective and subjective measures and that the effects of those objective measures on self-reported health could be very largely accounted for by the subjective measures. This has been reflected more recently in the work of various researchers (see, for example, Bosma & Marmot, 1997; Jex & Spector, 1996; Chen & Spector, 1991; Spector, 1987b). In French et al.'s study, objective occupation only accounted for some 2 to 6 percent of the variance in self-reported health beyond that accounted for by the subjective measures.

3.2.2 Demand-Control Model

Karasek (1979) drew attention to the possibility that work characteristics may not be linearly associated with worker health, and that they may combine interactively in relation to health. He initially demonstrated this theory through secondary analyses of data from United States and Sweden, finding that employees in jobs perceived to have both low decision latitude and high job demands[6] were particularly likely to re-

---

[6] Karasek (1979) defined 'decision latitude' as 'the working individual's potential control over his tasks and his conduct during the working day'. He defined 'job demands' as 'the psychological stressors involved in accomplishing the workload'.

port poor health and low satisfaction. Later studies appeared to confirm the theory. For example, a representative sample of Swedish working men was examined for depression, excessive fatigue, cardiovascular disease and mortality. Those workers whose jobs were characterised by heavy workloads combined with little latitude for decision making were represented disproportionately on all these outcome variables. The lowest probabilities for illness and death were found among work groups with moderate workloads combined with high control over work conditions (Ahlbom et al., 1977; Karasek, 1981; Karasek et al., 1981). The combined effect of these two work characteristics is often described as a true interaction, but despite the strong popular appeal of this suggestion there is only weak evidence in its support (Kasl, 1989; Warr, 1990). Karasek's (1979) own analyses suggest an additive rather than a synergistic effect, and he has admitted that "there is only moderate evidence for an interaction effect, understood as a departure from a linear additive model". Simple additive combinations have been reported by a number of researchers, for example, Hurrell & McLaney (1989), Payne & Fletcher (1983), Perrewe & Ganster (1989), and Spector (1987a).

Other criticisms have been levelled against Karasek's model. For instance, it was claimed that the model was too simple and ignores the moderating effect of social support on the main variables. Johnson (1989) and Johnson et al. (1991) expanded Karasek's model by adding a third dimension, resulting in the "Demand-Control-Support" model. The dimension "social support" refers to overall levels of helpful social interaction available on the job from both co-workers and supervisors. "Social support" seems to play an essential role in the management of stress at work. It serves as a buffer against possible adverse health affects of excessive psychological demands (Theorell, 1997). Johnson et al. (1991) distinguish between four types of low social support work situations and four of high social support. Winnubst & Schabracq (1996) found that high demands, low control and low support (high social isolation) were associated with an elevated cardiovascular risk. Most studies based on this model focus on *jobs*, i.e., broad occupational categories. Junghanns et al. (1999) applied the "Demand-Control-Support" model to specific conditions of work and confirmed that job characteristics such as decision latitude, psychological demands and social support affect health. They found that white-collar workers in "high-strain" work situations had the highest level of health complaints. Working situations characterised as highly demanding with low decision latitude and low social support predispose workers to experience health problems, especially musculoskeletal (shoulder and neck pain) and psychosomatic complaints (exhaustion, inner restlessness) (Ertel et al., 1997; Junghanns et al., 1999).

The expanded "Demand-Control-Support" model has also been criticised for its failure to consider individual differences in susceptibility and coping potential: The relationship between the dimensions of the model and the outcome measures may depend upon workers' individual characteristics (de Rijk et al., 1998). For instance, "disturbed relaxation ability" (also known as "inability to relax/work obsession") was found to be a valid predictor of increased sympathetic activation and delayed recovery of cardiovascular parameters. It reflects experienced intensity of work and job-related exhaustion (Richter et al., 1988, Richter et al., 1995). "Disturbed relaxation ability" relates to excessive work involvement, characterised by an extreme degree of work effort and by work "carry-over" into domestic life (to the extent of affecting sleep, relaxation and leisure, and neglecting personal needs). While a certain degree of work involvement can be considered "healthy" and stimulating, in its extreme form involvement can become 'work obsession' and lead to the inability to relax after work, with the risk of negative health effects (Rotheiler et al., 1997). "Disturbed relaxation ability" can moderate the health effects of the work-situations generated by the "Demand-Control-Support" model. Junghanns et al., (1998) found that high psychological demands and a high level of disturbed relaxation ability predispose workers to ill-health.

Finally, Carayon (1993) has offered four possible explanations for the inconsistency in the evidence concerning Karasek's model. First, the model seems to be supported in large, heterogeneous samples, but not in homogeneous samples: this may be due to the confounding effects of socio-economic status in heterogeneous samples or the lack of sensitivity of measures used in homogeneous samples. Second, inconsistencies may stem partly from the way job demands and decision latitude are conceptualised and measured. Karasek conceptualised decision latitude as a combination of decision authority (similar to control or autonomy) and skill discretion (similar to skill utilisation). Subsequent studies have included a wide variety of measures for decision latitude, and it is therefore possible that those that have used more focused measures are testing the effects of 'control' as opposed to the effects of 'decision latitude', which is a mixture of control and job complexity. Similarly, as far as 'demands' are concerned, the original measures tapped one main construct, 'workload', but subsequent studies have tended to employ a wider range of measures. Measures have varied considerably and are often far removed from Karasek's original formulation. Third, much of the research into this model relies on self-report measures of both dependent and independent variables; 'job satisfaction' is an example where there is content overlap between the measures. A related issue concerns the predominance of cross-sectional rather than longitudinal data, limiting interpretations as to cause and effect. Fourth, Carayon suggests there may be methodological and statistical reasons for the failure to find interactive effects. However, whether perceived job demands and decision latitude combine additively or through a true interaction, it is clear from Karasek's work that they are important factors determining the effects of work on employees' health.

3.3

TRANSACTIONAL
DEFINITIONS

Most transactional theories of stress focus on the cognitive processes and emotional reactions underpinning the person's interaction with their environment. For example, Siegrist's transactional model of "effort-reward imbalance" (Siegrist, 1990) argues that the experience of chronic stress can be best defined in terms of a mismatch between high costs spent and low gains received. In other words, according to the model, stress at work results from high effort spent in combination with low reward obtained. Two sources of effort are distinguished: an *extrinsic* source, the demands of the job, and an *intrinsic* source, the motivation of the individual worker in a demanding situation. Three dimensions of reward are important: financial gratifications, socio-emotional reward and status control (i.e., promotion prospects and job insecurity). Adverse health effects, such as cardiovascular risk,

are most prevalent in occupations where situational constraints prevent workers from reducing "high cost - low gain" conditions.

3.3.1 Theories of Appraisal and Coping

Most transactional models appear to build on the conceptual structures suggested in the interactional models of the Michigan school and Karasek and colleagues. They focus on the possible imbalance between demands and ability or competence. This is most obvious in the models advanced by Lazarus and Folkman in the United States (for example, Lazarus & Folkman, 1984) and Cox and Mackay in the United Kingdom (for example, Cox, 1978; Cox, 1990; Cox & Mackay, 1981). According to transactional models, stress is a negative *psychological state* [7] involving aspects of both cognition and emotion. They treat the stress state as the internal representation of particular and problematic transactions between the person and their environment.

Appraisal is the evaluative process that gives these person-environment transactions their meaning (Holroyd & Lazarus, 1982). Later refinements of the theory suggest both primary and secondary components to the appraisal process (Lazarus, 1966; Folkman & Lazarus, 1986). Primary appraisal involves a continual monitoring of the person's transactions with their en-

---

[7] The term *psychological stress* is ambiguous. While the experience of stress is psychological in nature, its antecedents and outcomes are not restricted to any particular domain, psychological or otherwise.

vironment (in terms of demands, abilities, competence, constraints and support), focusing on the question 'Do I have a problem?' The recognition of a problem situation is usually accompanied by unpleasant emotions or general discomfort. Secondary appraisal is contingent upon the recognition that a problem exists and involves a more detailed analysis and the generation of possible coping strategies: 'What am I going to do about it?'.

Stress arises when the person perceives that he or she cannot adequately cope with the demands being made on them or with threats to their well-being (Lazarus, 1966, 1976; Cox, 1990), when coping is of importance to them (Sells, 1970; Cox, 1978) and when they are anxious or depressed about it (Cox & Ferguson, 1991). The experience of stress is therefore defined by, first, the person's realisation that they are having difficulty coping with demands and threats to their well-being, and, second, that coping is important and the difficulty in coping worries or depresses them. This approach allows a clear distinction between, say, the effects of lack of ability on performance and those of stress. If a person does not have the necessary ability or competence –the knowledge or level of skill– to complete a task, then their performance will be poor. They may not realise this or if they do it might not be felt to be of importance or give rise to concern. These are not *stress scenarios*. However, if the person (a) does realise that they are failing to cope with the demands of a task, **and** (b) experiences concern about that failure because it is important, then this *is* a 'stress' scenario. The effects of

such stress might then cause a further impairment of performance over and above that caused by lack of ability.

The question of 'consciousness' has been raised in relation to stress and the appraisal process (Cox & Mackay, 1981). Appraisal is a conscious process. However, in its earliest stages, changes characteristic of the stress state may be demonstrated, yet the existence of a problem may not be recognised or recognition may only be 'hazy'. It has been suggested that different levels of awareness may exist during the appraisal process. These may be described by the following sequence:

1. Growing awareness of problem markers, both individual and situational, including feeling uncomfortable, not sleeping, making mistakes, etc.
2. Recognising the existence of a 'problem' in a general or 'hazy' way.
3. Identifying the general problem area and assessing its importance.
4. Analysing in detail the nature of the problem and its effects.

It is useful to think of the stress state as embedded in an *on-going process* that involves the person interacting with their environment, making appraisals of that interaction and attempting to cope with, and sometimes failing to cope with, the problems that arise. Cox (1978) described this process in terms of a five-stage model. The first stage, it was argued, represents the sources of demand faced by the person and is part of their environment. The person's perception of these demands in relation to their ability to cope represents the second stage: effectively primary appraisal. Consistent with Lazarus & Folkman

(Lazarus, 1966; Folkman & Lazarus, 1986) and French *et al.* (1982), stress was described as the psychological state that arose when there was a personally significant imbalance or lack of fit between the person's perceptions of the demands on them and their perceived ability to cope with those demands. The psychological and physiological changes which are associated with the recognition of such a stress state, and which include coping, represent the third stage of the model. Emotional changes are an important part of the stress state. These tend to be negative in nature and often define the experience of stress for the person. The fourth stage is concerned with the consequences of coping. The fifth stage is the general feedback (and feed forward) that occurs in relation to all other stages of the model. This model has been further developed in several ways. The importance of perceptions of control and of social support have been emphasised as factors in the appraisal process, and there has been some discussion of the problem of measuring stress based on this approach (Cox, 1985a, 1990) with the development of possible subjective measures of the experiential (mood) correlates of the stress state (see Mackay *et al.*, 1978; Cox & Mackay, 1985).

The experience of stress through work is therefore associated with exposure to particular conditions of work, both physical and psychosocial, and the worker's realisation that they are having difficulty in coping with important aspects of their work situation. The experience of stress is usually accompanied by attempts to deal with the underlying problem (coping) and by

changes in cognition, behaviour and physiological function (e.g., Aspinwall & Taylor, 1997; Guppy & Weatherstone, 1997). Although probably adaptive in the short term, such changes may threaten health in the long term. The experience of stress and its behavioural and psychophysiological correlates mediate[8], in part, the effects of many different types of work demand on health. This point has been made by many authors over the last three decades (for example, Levi, 1984; Szabo *et al.*, 1983; Scheck *et al.*, 1997).

---

[8] The mediator of a particular relationship, for example between stress and health, is a variable which effectively supplies the link between the two variables involved: it transmits the effects of one variable to the other.

3.4

SUMMARY: FRAMEWORKS,

THEORIES AND DEFINITIONS

Stress can be defined as a psychological state which is part of and reflects a wider process of interaction between the person and their work environment. It is concluded that there is a growing consensus around the adequacy and utility of the psychological approach to stress. Several overview models have been offered as summaries of the stress process. The most notable is that of Cooper (see, for example, Cooper & Marshall, 1976), as presented in Figure 2 below. Cooper's model usefully focuses on the nature and detail of work stresses and their individual and organisational outcomes.

Figure 2: Cooper's model of the dynamics of work stress (adapted from Cooper & Marshall, 1976)

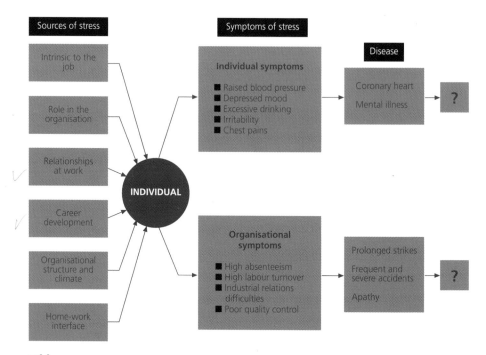

The stress state is a conscious state but the level of awareness of the problem varies with the development of that state. Part of the stress process are the relationships between the objective work environment and the employee's perceptions of work, between those perceptions and the experience of stress, and between that experience and changes in behaviour and physiological function, and in health. Coping is an important component of the stress process but one which is relatively poorly understood. Stress may be experienced as a result of exposure to a wide range of work demands and, in turn, contribute to an equally wide range of health outcomes: it is one link between hazards and health.

3.5

COPING

Coping is an important part of the overall stress process. However, it is perhaps the least well understood despite many years of research. This point is widely acknowledged in the literature (see, for example, Dewe et al., 1993, 2000) Lazarus (1966) has suggested that it has three main features. First, it is a *process*: it is what the person actually thinks and does in a stressful encounter. Second, it is *context-dependent*: coping is influenced by the particular encounter or appraisal that initiates it and by the resources available to manage that encounter. Finally, coping as a process is and should be defined *'independent of outcome'*; that is, independently of whether it was successful or not (see Folkman, 1984; Folkman et al., 1986a, 1986b; Lazarus & Folkman, 1984). There have been two approaches to the study of coping: that which attempts to classify the different types of coping strategies and

produce a comprehensive taxonomy, and that which considers coping as a problem-solving process (Dewe, 2000).

3.5.1 Coping Taxonomies

Lazarus (1966) has argued that the person usually employs both task and emotion focused coping strategies. The former attempt some form of action directly targeted at dealing with the source of stress (adaptation *of* the environment), while the latter attempt to attenuate the emotional experience associated with that stress (adaptation *to* the environment). The perceived success, or otherwise, of such strategies feeds back into the appraisal process to alter the person's perception of the situation. Lazarus and his colleagues (Lazarus, 1966; Lazarus & Folkman, 1984) also emphasise that the importance of the situation to the individual is critical in determining the intensity of their response.

Dewe (1987), in a typical study, examined sources of stress and strategies used to cope with them in ministers of religion in New Zealand. Using factor analytical techniques, he identified five clusters of coping strategies: seeking social support, postponing action by relaxation and distracting attention, developing greater ability to deal with the problem, rationalising the problem, and drawing on support through spiritual commitment. It was possible to classify 33% of the strategies which made up these clusters as *task focused* and 67% as *emotion focused*. The most frequent source of stress experienced by the ministers related to the emotional and time difficulties associated with crisis work, and the experience of such problems appeared to be associated with coping by seeking social support and rationalising the problem.

Pearlin and associates (Pearlin & Schooler, 1978; Pearlin *et al.*, 1981) have further developed this general approach and distinguished between responses concerned with changing the situation, those concerned with changing its meaning (re-appraisal) and those relating to the management of the symptoms of stress. In a different vein, Miller (1979; Miller *et al.*, 1988) has distinguished between two informational styles which she terms 'blunters' and 'monitors': the former tend to use denial strategies and the latter information seeking strategies in relation to stressful situations.

These and the many other classifications available in the literature are, generally, neither inconsistent nor meant to be mutually exclusive. Most authors emphasise that no one type of coping strategy is necessarily better than any other in solving a problem. People use a mixture of strategies in most situations, although certain situations may tend to be associated with particular types of strategy. Some studies have tried to explore the existence of systematic links between stressors and coping styles, but found little empirical support for their hypotheses. Salo (1995) found differences in teachers' ways of coping, but those differences related to the amount, not the source, of stress experienced, and the timing (changed throughout the autumn term). Wykes & Whittington (1991) studied the different ways in which psychiatric nursing staff

dealt with incidents of violent physical assault. They found that each respondent reported an average three distinct coping strategies. These studies seem to support the existence of complex, dynamic and context-dependent coping behaviours, rather than causally driven schemata of coping. Furthermore, although in theory Lazarus' model allows for environmental feedback to alter the perceptions –and, hence, perhaps to determine future coping– in practice his taxonomy is rather static and emphasises coping *styles*, whilst tending to ignore coping *behaviours* (Dewe *et al.*, 1993).

3.5.2 Coping as Problem-solving

Coping can also be viewed as a problem-solving strategy (Cox, 1987; Fisher, 1986; Dewe, 1993; Aspinwall & Taylor, 1997). Cox (1987), for example, has described a cycle of activities, beginning with recognition and diagnosis (analysis) followed by actions and evaluation through to re-analysis, which possibly represents the ideal problem-solving process. However, Schonpflug & Battmann (1988) have emphasised that by adopting the wrong actions, or by failing, a person may create further problems and stress. At the same time, Meichenbaum (1977) argues that 'catastrophizing' or reacting too strongly to such failure serves no adaptive purpose and it is often said that one of the few positive aspects to coping with stress is that the person learns from such experience. However, Einhorn & Hogarth (1981) suggest that there are at least three problems with this proposition: first, one does not necessarily know that there is something to be learned, second, what is to be learned is not clear, and third, there is ambiguity in judging whether one has learned. Furthermore, the *problem solver* may be fully occupied and not have any spare cognitive capacity for learning, and the emotion associated with stress may interfere with the learning process (Mandler, 1982).

Coping may be seen as functional in its attempts to manage demands, by either changing them, redefining them (re-appraisal) or adapting to them. The styles and strategies used need to be relevant and applicable to the situation at hand. The choice and successful use of these responses will be determined by both the nature of the situation, by the personal and social resources available and also by the type of causal reasoning adopted in the appraisal process.

3.6

INDIVIDUAL AND GROUP DIFFERENCES

Most contemporary theories of stress allow for individual differences in the experience of stress, and in how and how well it is coped with. In 1988, Payne presented a series of questions, including:

• How do individual differences relate to perceptions of stress in the work environment?

• Do they affect the way people cope with stress?

• Do they act as moderators of the stress-health relationship?

• How do individual differences, such as competence and work ability, relate to the development of ill health?

There would appear to be two different approaches to research on individual differences based on Payne's (1988) questions. Effectively individual difference variables have been investigated as either: (1) components of the appraisal process,

or (2) moderators[9] of the stress-health relationship (see Cox & Ferguson, 1991). Hence, researchers have asked, for example, to what extent are particular workers vulnerable to the experience of stress, or to what extent does, say, 'hardiness' (Kobasa, 1979; Kobasa & Pucetti, 1983; Kobasa et al., 1981, 1982) moderate the relationship between job characteristics and worker health?

This distinction between individual differences as components of the appraisal process and moderators of the stress-outcome relationship can be easily understood in terms of transactional models of stress (e.g., Cox & Griffiths, 1996).

Primary appraisal is, by its very nature, subject to individual differences. First, individual differences may exist in relation to the person's perception of job demands and pressures. Kahn (1974), for example, found a modest relationship between objective and subjective measures of role conflict. The objective measure was based on the sum of pressures to change behaviour as reported by those who had formal influence on the person in the role in question. Further analyses revealed that this relationship largely resulted from those in the sample who were high on anxiety proneness. Anxiety proneness appeared to moderate the person's perception of role conflict. In the same vein, Payne & Hartley

---

[9] A moderator of a particular relationship, say between stress and health, is a variable which may alter the strength or direction of that relationship. The technical concept of moderation implies no particular direction of effect although in every day usage it tends to imply a weakening of effect.

(1987) found a positive correlation be-tween perceptions of the severity of prob-lems facing unemployed men and a measure of locus of control. The more they believed that important life events were not under their personal control, the more severe they perceived their problems to be. Second, people vary in their ability to cope with demands, and in their perceptions of those abilities. Such variation may be a function of their intelligence, their experi-ence and education, or their beliefs in their ability to cope (self efficacy: Bandura, 1977; job self-efficacy: Schaubroeck & Merritt, 1997). Third, people may vary in the amount of control that they can exer-cise over any situation, not only as a func-tion of that situation but also as a function of their beliefs about control. Fourth, peo-ple may vary in their need for social sup-port and the skills that they have for exploiting such support, and in their per-ceptions of support. Finally, the stress-health relationship is obviously moderated by individual differences not only in sec-ondary appraisal but also in coping behav-iour and emotional and physiological response tendencies, latencies and pat-terns.

3.6.1 Type A Behaviour

Over the last 30 years, much attention has focused on individual vulnerability in rela-tion to coronary heart disease and on the role of psychological and behavioural fac-tors in reacting to and coping with stress-ful situations. The concept of type A behaviour was originally developed as a description of overt behaviour by Friedman & Rosenman (1974) but has since been considerably broadened and, some have argued, weakened as a result (Arthur *et al.*, 1999; Powell, 1987). Friedman & Rosenman (1974) described *type A behav-iour* as a major behavioural risk factor for cardiovascular ill health. There are at least three characteristics that mark out the type A individual whose risk of coronary heart disease appears, from studies in the Unit-ed States, to be at least twice that of the non type A:

• A strong commitment to work and much involvement in their job
• A well developed sense of time urgency (always aware of time pressures and working against deadlines)
• A strong sense of competition and a marked tendency to be aggressive

Such behaviour is probably learnt, and is often valued by and maintained through particular organisational cultures.

There is some confusion in the literature as to the status of the behaviours referred to above and their relative importance and that of related constructs. Some refer to type A behaviour as a learnt style of be-haviour, others as a coping pattern, and still others as a personality trait (Powell, 1987). At the same time, there have been various suggestions as to its most impor-tant dimension. For example, Glass (1977) has argued that control is the determining factor, while Williams *et al.* (1985) and others have argued in favour of hostility or aggression (see for example, Dembroski *et al.*, 1985; MacDougal *et al.*, 1985), and others for low self esteem (Friedman & Ul-mer, 1984). Various different measures have been developed, not all of which strongly inter-relate (e.g.: Arthur *et al.*,

1999; Powell, 1987), thus questioning their operational precision and construct validity.

Perhaps of the three, the two that have attracted most attention are (i) control and (ii) anger and hostility.

Control

The issue of control is important in understanding the nature of type A behaviour. The type A individual feels that they are always fighting to maintain control over events, which are often seen to be just beyond their grasp. Faced with these situations, they simply expend more time and effort trying to "get events under control" –and never really feel as if they have succeeded (Glass & Singer, 1972). The issue of control, and of being in control, is an important one and may distinguish between the vulnerability of type As and the resistance of hardy types (Kobasa, 1979; Weinberg *et al.*, 1999; Kobasa & Pucetti, 1983; Kobasa *et al.*, 1981, 1982). Kobasa's hardy types report feeling in control of their work and their lives. Type A behaviour predicts cardiovascular ill health, while hardiness predicts general good health.

Anger & Hostility

Indices of anger and hostility have been validated in prospective research as predictors of cardiovascular ill health. For example, Matthews *et al.* (1977) scored 10 responses to the Structured Interview for type A behaviour (see Jenkins *et al.*, 1968) of 186 cases and controls in the Western Group Collaborative Study (see, for example, Rosenman *et al.*, 1964a and 1964b).

Seven of the 10 responses discriminated between the cases and controls and the majority of these related to anger and hostility. Others have also found evidence suggesting that measures of hostility, repressed hostility or potential for hostility can strongly predict cardiovascular health (Dembroski *et al.*, 1985; Arthur *et al.*, 1999; MacDougall *et al.*, 1985; Williams *et al.*, 1980; Barefoot *et al.*, 1983; Shekelle *et al.*, 1983). Perez *et al.* (1999) have recently found that *expression of anger* discriminated between coronary patients on the one hand, and non-coronary patients and healthy people on the other.

The relationship between type A behaviour and cardiovascular health is potentially moderated by a host of factors such as age, sex, socio-economic and educational status, employment status, medication and the cardiovascular outcome chosen for study (Powell, 1987). Interestingly, Kittel and his colleagues (1983) have concluded that there are also marked differences between studies in the United States and those in Europe. The results from Europe do not appear to have fulfilled the early promise of those conducted in the United States. There may be sociolinguistic and cultural differences which affect either the validity of the measuring instruments or the validity or role of the concept (e.g., Lu *et al.*, 1999; Martinez & Martos, 1999; Mudrack, 1999; Kawakami & Haratani, 1999).

3.6.2 Vulnerable Groups

Individual differences are obvious in the stress process affecting appraisal and coping mechanisms, and the stress-health relationship. Group differences –and the creation of vulnerable groups– may represent the effects of individual differences which are common to, and characteristic of, particular groups, and/or the effects of common patterns of exposure to hazardous work conditions (or some combination of the two; see, for example, Weinberg *et al.*'s (1999) study of British Members of Parliament). Several different reviews have identified possible vulnerable groups (see, for example, Levi, 1984; Davidson & Earnshaw, 1991) including: young workers, older workers, migrant workers, disabled workers and women workers. Kasl (1992) has attempted to summarise the different criteria and factors that define vulnerability as: socio-demography (for example, age and educational status), social status (for example, living alone), behavioural style (type A behaviour), skills and abilities, health status and medical history, and ongoing non-work problems. Such vulnerability factors are moderators of the hazard-stress-harm relationship and probably interact in defining the high risk or vulnerable groups mentioned above.

The recognition of the vulnerability of such groups is not new and, in the United Kingdom, its origins can be traced back to the earliest health and safety legislation as, for example, in the Health & Morals of Apprentices Act of 1802.

3.6.3 Selection

The individual and group differences have been highlighted in relation to the experience and health effects of stress. Such differences may be treated in a number of ways depending as much on moral and legal as on scientific considerations. Excluding particular workers or types of worker from work, which is judged to be stressful, may appear, at first sight, to be scientifically justified, but may not be legally sanctionable under the Equal Opportunities legislation in the EU Member States, or morally acceptable if other approaches are possible.

Furthermore, although individual differences can be shown to moderate the hazard-stress-health process, the evidence is not strong enough to support the design of defensible selection procedures. There appears to be little evidence of trait-like vulnerability to stress beyond that implied for psychological health by a personal or family history of related psychological disorders. Evidence for the apparent existence of any such traits may simply reflect commonly occurring patterns of *person x environment* interactions. Alternative strategies, focused on the design of jobs and organisation of work are available and more defensible given current knowledge of the relationship between work hazards and stress. Equally, approaches based on worker education and training and on enhanced support for workers in order to increase their work ability are also possible, and have been tried and evaluated.

3.7

SUMMARY: INDIVIDUAL DIFFERENCES – WORK ABILITY AND COPING

The experience of stress is partly dependent on the individual's ability to cope with the demands placed on them by their work, and on the way in which they subsequently cope with those demands, and related issues of control and support. More information is required on the nature, structure and effectiveness of individuals' abilities to meet work demands and to cope with any subsequent stress. The need for more information on coping is widely recognised (see, for example, Dewe, 2000), but relatively less attention has been paid to the need better to understand the concept of work ability or competence, although this is being flagged in relation to ageing research (e.g., Griffiths, 1999a; Ilmarinen & Rantanen, 1999)

RESEARCH

4.

METHODOLOGICAL ISSUES

4.1

MEASUREMENT

It has been suggested that the available evidence supports a psychological approach to the definition of stress, and that transactional models are among the most adequate and useful of those currently available. Within this framework, stress is defined as a psychological state (see section 3.1.3) which is both part of and reflects a wider process of interaction between the person and their (work) environment. This process is based on a sequence of relationships between the objective work environment and the worker's perceptions, between those perceptions and the experience of stress, and between that experience, changes in behaviour and physiological function, and health. This sequence provides a basis for measurement, but the different measures which can be derived from the sequence cannot be easily or defensibly combined into a single stress index (see below).

Logically the measurement of the stress state must be based primarily on self-report measures which focus on the appraisal process and on the emotional experience of stress (Cox, 1985a; Cox & Ferguson, 1994). Measures relating to appraisal need to consider the worker's perceptions of the demands on them, their ability to cope with those demands, their needs and the extent to which they are fulfilled by work, the control they have over work and the support they receive in relation to work. Dewe (1991) has argued that it is necessary to go beyond simply asking workers whether particular demands, etc. are present (or absent) in their work environments and measure various dimensions of demand such as frequency, duration and level. Furthermore, such measures need to be used in a way which allows for the possibility of interactions between perceptions, such as demand with control (Karasek, 1979; Warr, 1990) or demand and control with support (Payne & Fletcher, 1983; Cox, 1985a; Karasek & Theorell, 1990). The importance to the worker of coping with particular combinations and expressions of these work characteristics needs also to be taken into account (Sells, 1970; Cox, 1978).

4.2

SELF-REPORT DATA AND TRIANGULATION

Since the most readily available data on psychosocial and organisational hazards of work are usually the self-reports of those involved in the work under consideration, eliciting and modelling the knowledge and perceptions of employees is central to the assessment process. Despite their obvious centrality and importance, self-report measures of appraisal and the emotional experience of stress are, on their own, insufficient. While their reliability can be established in terms of their internal structure or performance over time without reference to other data, their validity cannot.

The validity of self-report data has been questioned in particular with regard to the issue of "negative affectivity" (e.g. Heinisch & Jex, 1998; Kristensen, 1996; Beehr, 1995; Sheffield et al. 1994; Frese & Zapf, 1988). Negative affectivity (NA) can

be defined as "a general personality trait reflecting individual differences in negative emotionality and self-concept, i.e., concentrating on negative aspects of everything and experiencing considerable distress in all situations" (Watson & Clark, 1984). NA would affect not only workers' perception of their work environment, but also their appraisal of their own psychological health status or well-being, thus becoming a confounding variable that could account for a large proportion of the correlations between perceived hazards and perceived outcomes. Kasl (1987) referred to this methodological weakness when he wrote about *the triviality trap* (i.e., some researchers' reliance on trivial correlations that can be explained away by common method variance): "The sheer volume of studies which has been generated by cross-sectional retrospective designs, in which only self-reports of independent, intervening, and outcome variables are correlated to each other, is so enormous that they have created their own standard of "acceptable methodology" Kasl, 1987).

The research literature is still divided on the extent to which NA or common method variance distort the assessment of the stress-strain relationship (e.g., Jex & Spector, 1996; Stansfeld et al., 1995; Heinisch & Jex, 1998). However, there are ways in which the design of assessment instruments and procedures can contribute to ensuring that the data obtained are of good quality. It is clear that an assessment relying solely on appraisal would represent very weak evidence, and would need to be supported by data from other domains. *Tri-*

angulation[10] of evidence overcomes the potential problems of NA to some extent (Jick, 1979; Cox & Ferguson, 1994). The principle of triangulation holds that, to be secure, a potential psychosocial or organisational hazard must be identified by cross-reference to at least three different types of evidence. The degree of agreement between those different points of view provides some indication of the reliability of the data and, depending on the measures used, their concurrent validity. Applying this principle would require data to be collected from at least three different domains (Cox, 1990). This can be achieved by considering evidence relating to [1] the objective and subjective antecedents of the person's experience of stress, [2] their self-report of stress, and [3] any changes in their behaviour, physiology or health status[11] which might be correlated with [1] and/or [2]. The influence of moderating factors, such as individual and group differences (see section 3.6), may also be assessed.

Several authors have recommended measurement strategies that are consistent with the concept of triangulation. For example, Kristensen (1996) proposes a "3-S matrix" which would apply the principles of triangulation to the three main elements of the 'stress equation' (stressors, stress and sickness). Bailey & Bhagat (1987) have recommended a multi-method approach to the measurement of stress. They have argued in favour of balancing the evidence from self-report, physiological and unobtrusive measures. Their unobtrusive measures relate to what Folger & Belew (1985) and Webb *et al.* (1966) have called non-reactive measures, and include: physical traces (such as poor house keeping), archival data (such as that on absenteeism), private records (such as diaries), and non intrusive observation and recordings. Bailey & Bhagat (1987) also point up the problem that obtrusive measures often change the very nature of the behaviour or other response being assessed. It is also necessary to devise standardised procedures for the corroboration, or otherwise, of qualitative data with quantitative measures, and between sets of qualitative data from different sources.

Confidence on the validity of the data thus obtained is supported by various studies which have shown that there is good convergence between self-report and supervisor- and subordinate-report (e.g. Bosma & Marmot, 1997; Jex & Spector, 1996; Spector *et al.*, 1988).

Triangulation would require evidence drawn from an audit of the work environment (including both its physical and its psychosocial aspects: see sections 5.1 and 5.2), from a survey of workers' perceptions of and reactions to work, from the measurement of workers' behaviour in respect to work, and their physiological and health status (see section 6). It is not possible here to offer a comprehensive review of the plethora of measures which might be used in such audits and surveys. However, section 5 suggests the various physical and

[10] The concept of triangulation in measurement relates to the strategy of fixing a particular position or finding by examining it from at least three different points of view.

[11] The changes in behaviour, physiology and health status which may be correlated with the antecedents and/or experience of stress are discussed in section 6.

psychosocial antecedents of stress that might be measured in the workplace, while the measurement of the stress state has been outlined above. Measures of the third domain (behaviour, physiology and health status) are well established in the general literature on occupational psychology and psychophysiology. The use of any measure must be supported by data relating to its reliability and validity, and its appropriateness and fairness in the situation in which it is being used. The provision of such data would conform to good practice in both occupational psychology and psychometrics (e.g., Cox & Ferguson, 1994), but may also be required if any subsequent decisions are challenged in law. Preferably such data collection would take the form of continuous monitoring and thus be capable of mapping work-related changes in all three domains.

Ideally, the principle of triangulation should be applied both within and between domains. This should help overcome the problem of missing data and help resolve inconsistencies in the data given that these are not extreme. Its use between domains has been briefly discussed above. Within domains, several different measures should be taken and preferably across different measurement modalities to avoid problems of common method variance. This may be most relevant and easiest to achieve in relation to the measurement of changes in the third domain: behaviour, physiology and health status. There are no available studies to suggest that the various measures from the different domains can be statistically combined into a single and defensible 'stress index'.

It needs to be emphasised that what is being measured is *a process*: antecedents – perceptions and experience (and moderating factors) – immediate outcomes – health status. This approach underlines both the complexity of measurement, when approached scientifically, and the inadequacy of asking for or using single one-off measures of *stress* (however defined). This process can be simplified conceptually to '[work] hazards – stress – harm', and this is the framework used to structure the evidence relating to work stress and health in the following sections of this Status Report. This has the practical advantage of placing the issue of occupational stress within a framework familiar to those working with health and safety problems and consistent with recent European legislation. The following sections of this Report consider work hazards and stress (section 5), and stress and health (section 6).

4.3

SUMMARY

viewed a number of "triangulation" strategies that researchers have adopted to that end, and has highlighted the need to develop standardised procedures for the corroboration of qualitative data with quantitative measures, and between sets of qualitative data from different sources. Finally, it must be noted that the concepts of *process* and *interaction* have important implications for the operationalisation of stress theory: the measurement of the "stress process" is, when approached scientifically, unavoidably complex and not adequately addressed by single one-off measures. The following sections of this Report describe a framework for the assessment and management of work-related stress that aims to reflect the dynamic nature of the process.

Previous sections have examined the evidence that supports the transactional models of stress as the most adequate and useful of those currently available. Within this framework, work-related stress is defined as a psychological state that is both part of and reflects a wider process of interaction between the person and their work environment. It follows that the measurement of stress must be based primarily on self-report measures which focus on the appraisal process, the emotional experience and the person-environment interaction. However, such self-report measures are, on their own, insufficient, and there has been much debate on the methodological problems posed by "negative affectivity" and common method variance. The existing literature has identified the need to establish the validity of self-report data with reference to additional, external evidence. This section has re-

RESEARCH

competencies and needs on the other. Those interactions which prove hazardous influence employees' health through their perceptions and experience (International Labour Organization, 1986). While this definition is consistent with transactional models of stress, it associates exposure to psychosocial hazards too strongly with the experience of stress. It is argued here that psychosocial hazards may also have direct effects on the person, effects which are not mediated by the experience of stress. As a result, a more satisfactory definition of psychosocial hazards might be "those aspects of work design and the organisation and management of work, and their social and environmental contexts, which have the potential for causing psychological, social or physical harm" (Cox & Griffiths, 1995).

Exposure to physical and psychosocial hazards may affect psychological as well as physical health. The evidence suggests that such effects on health may be mediated by, at least, two processes (see Figure 3 below): first, a direct physical pathway, and second, a psychological stress-mediated pathway. These two mechanisms do not offer alternative explanations of the hazard-health association; in most hazardous situations both operate and interact to varying extents and in various ways (Levi, 1984; Cox & Cox, 1993). Levi (1984) has noted that both additive and synergistic interactions[12] are possible.

5.

WORK HAZARDS AND STRESS

In line with both the scientific literature and current legislation, this Report considers the evidence relating to all work hazards. These can be broadly divided into *physical hazards* (section 5.1), which include the biological, biomechanical, chemical and radiological, and *psychosocial hazards* (section 5.2).

The International Labour Organization (1986) has defined psychosocial hazards in terms of the interactions among job content, work organisation and management, environmental and organisational conditions, on the one hand, and the employees'

---

[12] The outcome of effects that interact additively is simply the sum of the separate effects; however, the outcome of effects that interact synergistically is other than the sum of the separate effects. It may be greater, where one set of effects facilitates or enhances another, or it may be smaller, where one set attenuates or weakens another.

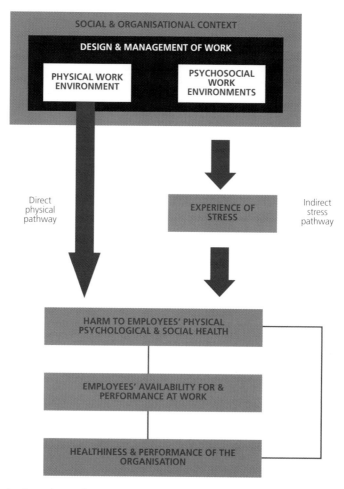

Figure 3: The dual pathway hazard – harm

Many of the existing discussions of the hazard-*stress*-health relationship have focused on psychosocial hazards and have tended to omit reference to physical work hazards (Levi, 1984). The psychological effects of physical hazards reflect not only their direct action on the brain and their unpleasantness but also the worker's awareness, suspicion or fear that they are being exposed to harm. It is the latter which can give rise to the experience of stress. For example, exposure to organic solvents may have a psychological effect on the worker through their direct effects on the brain, through the unpleasantness of their smell and through the worker's fear that such exposure might be harmful (Levi, 1981; Kasl, 1992). Such fear may have consequences for task performance as well as for health [13]. The psychological effects of similar agents, carcinogens and toxic materials, appear dependent on the information available to and the awareness of workers (Houts & MacDougall, 1988). The prevalence of stressful physical environments cannot be ignored, and it has been reported to be on the increase across the EU between 1991 and 1996 (European Foundation, 1996).

Concern for occupational stress therefore focuses on two scenarios: first, the stress associated with exposure to the physical hazards of work (section 5.1), and, second, the stress which arises from exposure to psychosocial hazards (section 5.2).

---

[13] While low levels of anxiety and fear may have a motivating quality, higher levels can impair task performance (see, for example, M. Eysenck, 1983; Idzikowski & Baddeley, 1983) as well as impairing the quality of life. Deterioration in performance can be expected in tasks involving manual dexterity and sensory-motor coordination, such as tracking, in complex cognitive tasks and in secondary tasks. Some of these effects may be mediated by impairments of memory processes, and some by an increase in task-irrelevant and intrusive thoughts. The performance effects of anxiety and fear may increase with task difficulty. Deterioration in secondary task performance is likely to occur before performance of the primary task is affected. Baddeley (1972) has suggested that dangerous situations which are emotionally arousing may affect performance by a narrowing of attention which may cause peripheral stimuli to be missed. Together these different effects may interfere with the safeness of working practices.

5.1

PHYSICAL HAZARDS

A wide variety of physical hazards have been extensively studied for their effects on the psychological experience of stress and on health (see, for example, Gobel *et al.*, 1998; United States Department of Health, 1980; Holt, 1982; Neale *et al.*, 1983). Most can be measured objectively, and with some degree of reliability and validity, and are therefore relatively easily monitored in the workplace. In some cases, standards exist which can be used in the regulation of exposure to these potential sources of harm. Particular attention has been paid to noise as a source of stress and threat to health (Holt, 1982), and this is taken here as an exemplar of physical hazards.

5.1.1 Noise

Noise can act as a physical and a psychological stimulus (Akerstedt & Landstrom,

1998; Kryter, 1972; Kasl, 1992). Smith (1991) suggests that "the (non auditory) health effects of noise may often reflect psychological reactions to the noise -stress- as well as objective exposure levels". High levels of noise directly damage the middle and inner ears with consequent impairment of hearing (Jones, 1983). Less severe noise may interfere with speech perception and communication (Jones, 1999) and, particularly if it is prolonged, may give rise to the experience of stress, and to anxiety, irritability and tension, increase fatigue and impair performance efficiency (see, for example, Cohen, 1969, 1974; Barreto *et al.*, 1997; Glass & Singer, 1972; Miller, 1974; Cohen, 1980; Ahasan *et al.*, 1999). However, Jones (1983) has concluded that evidence of the relationship between noise and psychological and physical health (beyond damage to the ear and hearing impairment) is equivocal: while health effects have been found in a number of studies, they cannot be unequivocally linked to exposure to high levels of noise. He argues that in most studies the effects of noise are confounded with those of other hazards: noisy work is often hazardous in other respects. While such arguments are valid, they do need to be placed in perspective given the complexity of all work design and the availability of other data (e.g., Landstrom *et al.*, 1995). Smith (1991) has concluded that there is considerable evidence that acute noise exposure produces physiological responses which, if prolonged, could have harmful effects on health. He has also argued that the available epidemiological data suggest that noise is a risk factor for health. Furthermore, intervention and epidemiological studies suggest that noise can have harmful effects on health (see, for example, Cohen, 1976; Wallhagen et al., 1997). As with most occupational health issues, it is a case of integrating different types of evidence in reaching a balanced conclusion.

Cohen (1974) examined the effects of noise on absence from work due to illness, on accidents and on diagnosed medical problems over a five-year period in two major plants. Data were collected from plant records. One plant manufactured large boilers and the other manufactured electronic missile and weapon components. Workers drawn from high noise areas (95 dBA or more) were compared to workers drawn from low noise areas (80 dBA or less). Those from the high noise areas exhibited a higher incidence of problems on all measures. Especially prevalent in those exposed to high noise were allergies, respiratory and gastrointestinal disorders and complaints associated with musculo-skeletal and cardiovascular conditions. However, larger differences in the incidence of these problems appeared when they were compared by job type (rather than noise), and although attempts were made to control for job type in the analysis of noise effects these were not entirely successful (Jones, 1983). If noise was of aetiological significance, then its effects appeared to be less than –or secondary to– those of job design and work organisation. However, the noise effects were not insignificant and a follow up study by Cohen (1976) found evidence of a reduction in accident rate and incidence of medical problems as a result of introducing ear defenders.

5.1.2 Other Physical Factors

Overall, there is much evidence to suggest that poor physical working conditions, in general, can affect both workers' experience of stress and their psychological and physical health (Warr, 1992). However, there are few studies which directly establish the hazard-stress-harm pathway. Some studies have suggested that the effects of physical hazards on the experience of stress and on health are not related. Althouse & Hurrell (1977), for example, compared 486 coal miners in the United States with 452 workers in jobs of similar status. Despite a difference in the levels of physical dangerousness of the two types of work (exposure of workers to possible injury and death), there were no differences in experience of stress although miners did report significantly more symptoms of ill health such as irritation and somatic complaints.

In the case of some hazards, such as temperature and humidity (Biersner et al., 1971), it is the extremes of physical work conditions which are associated with the experience of stress and with effects on health: workers are often able to adapt to mid-range conditions without effort or attention (Holt, 1982; Szabo et al., 1983). In the case of others it is more simply the presence of the hazard or even the perceived threat of its presence which is associated with the experience of stress. An example is provided by doctors' and nurses' reports of anxiety in relation to dealing with patients who might be infected with the human immunodeficiency virus (Kegeles et al., 1989; Cox et al., 1993). Physical hazards not only interact with one and another in producing their effects, but may also interact with psychosocial hazards (e.g., Melamed *et al.*, 1999; Schrijvers *et al.*, 1998). Broadbent (1971) has described how noise and sleep loss might interact in relation to task performance, while there is other evidence that exposure to poor equipment and work station design, in conjunction with poor task design and work organisation give rise to work-related upper limb disorders (Chatterjee, 1987, 1992: Health & Safety Executive, 1990a).

5.2

PSYCHOSOCIAL HAZARDS

The psychological aspects of work have been the subject of research since at least the 1950s (Johnson, 1996; Sauter et al., 1998). Initially psychologists concentrated mostly on the obstacles to employees' adaptation and adjustment to the work environment, rather than on the potentially hazardous characteristics the workplace itself may have for workers (Gardell, 1982). However, with the emergence of psychosocial work environment research and occupational psychology in the 1960s (Johnson & Hall, 1996) the focus of interest has moved away from an individual perspective and towards considering the impact of certain aspects of the work environment on health. As suggested earlier, "psychosocial hazards" can be defined as "those aspects of work design and the organisation and management of work, and their social and environmental contexts, which have the potential for causing psy-

chological or physical harm" (Cox & Griffiths, 1995). There is now a large body of evidence (e.g., Cox, 1993; Landy et al., 1994; Kasl, 1987 & 1990) that identifies a common set of work characteristics as potentially hazardous (see Table 1).

Psychosocial hazards may affect both psychological and physical health directly or indirectly through the experience of stress (see Figure 3). Most attention has been paid to their possible indirect, stress-mediated effects. It is this literature which is reviewed below.

Work situations are experienced as stressful when they are perceived as involving important work demands which are not well matched to the knowledge and skills (competencies) of workers or their needs, especially when those workers have little control over work and receive little support at work (see section 5.2.1). Levi (1984) has grouped the various psychosocial characteristics of work under four headings which can be derived from this model: quantitative overload, qualitative underload, lack of control over work and lack of social support. Each aspect of such work situations carries a potential for harm and thus represents a hazard. These are the fundamental dimensions of psychosocial hazards in that they underpin the person's perception of the stressfulness of any work situation. They may, however, find 'surface' expression and combine in different ways for different hazards depending on the type of work and work environment.

There is a reasonable consensus among the various attempts to review the literature on those psychosocial hazards of

67

work which are experienced as stressful and/or otherwise carry the potential for harm (Baker, 1985; Blohmke & Reimer, 1980; Cooper & Marshall, 1976; Cox, 1978, 1985b; Cox & Cox, 1993; Frankenhauser & Gardell, 1976; Karasek & Theorell, 1990; Kasl, 1992; Levi, 1972, 1984; Levi et al., 1986; Loher et al., 1985; Marmot & Madge, 1987; National Institute, 1988; Sauter et al., 1992; Sharit & Salvendy, 1982; Szabo et al., 1983; Warr, 1987, 1992). This consensus is summarised in , which outlines ten different categories of job characteristics, work environments and organisations which may be hazardous. It has been suggested (Hacker, 1991; Hacker et al., 1983) that such characteristics of work might be usefully conceived as relating to the *context* to work or the *content* of work. Under certain conditions each of these ten aspects of work has proved stressful and harmful to health: these conditions are also noted in . Much of the evidence relates to psychological health and to the risk of cardiovascular disease (see section 6).

Table 1: Stressful Characteristics of Work

Category	Conditions defining hazard
Context to work	
Organisational culture and function	Poor communication, low levels of support for problem-solving and personal development, lack of definition of organisational objectives.
Role in organisation	Role ambiguity and role conflict, responsibility for people.
Career development	Career stagnation and uncertainty, underpromotion or overpromotion, poor pay, job insecurity, low social value to work.
Decision latitude / Control	Low participation in decision making, lack of control over work (control, particularly in the form of participation, is also a context and wider organisational issue)
Interpersonal relationships at work	Social or physical isolation, poor relationships with superiors, interpersonal conflict, lack of social support.
Home-work interface	Conflicting demands of work and home, low support at home, dual career problems.
Content of work	
Work environment and work equipment	Problems regarding the reliability, availability, suitability and maintenance or repair of both equipment and facilities.
Task design	Lack of variety or short work cycles, fragmented or meaningless work, underuse of skills; high uncertainty.
Workload / workpace	Work overload or underload, lack of control over pacing, high levels of time pressure.
Work schedule	Shift working, inflexible work schedules, unpredictable hours, long or unsocial hours.

5.2.1 Context to Work

The following section describes those psychosocial hazards which are related to the "context to work" and which are experienced as stressful and/or otherwise carry the potential for harm.

Organisational Culture and Function

The very fact of working within an organisation, as do most workers in Europe (Cox et al., 1990), can be perceived as a threat to individual freedom, autonomy and identity (Hingley & Cooper, 1986). Studies on employees' perceptions and descriptions of their organisations suggest that these revolve around three distinct aspects of organisational function and culture: the organisation as a task environment, as a problem-solving environment and as a development environment (Cox & Howarth, 1990; Cox & Leiter, 1992). The available evidence suggests that if the organisation is perceived to be poor in respect to these environments, then this is likely to be associated with increased levels of stress. On the other hand, if the organisation is perceived to be good in these respects then the relationship between the experience of stress and the report of symptoms of ill health is attenuated (Cox & Kuk, 1991).

Kasl (1992) has listed various aspects of organisation which he believes may be hazardous; for example, organisational size and structure (having a flat structure with relatively few levels), cumbersome and arbitrary procedures, and role-related issues. The latter are dealt with below. Much of the effect of organisation and function

and culture on workers will be transmitted through the behaviour of managers and supervisors. There is evidence, for example, that management behaviour and supervisory styles have a substantial impact on the emotional well-being of workers (Landy, 1992; Corey & Wolf, 1992). Such an influence may be partly a reflection of their handling of the job context and job content issues listed in . Following this argument, any effect of style might be largely a reflection of more general issues of interpersonal relationships.

Role in Organisation

The evidence that 'role in organisation' is a potential psychosocial hazard relates largely to issues of role ambiguity and role conflict (Kahn et al., 1964; Kahn, 1973; Ingersoll et al., 1999; Jackson & Schuler, 1985). However, other potentially hazardous aspects of role have been identified including role overload, role insufficiency and responsibility for other people (see below). French et al. (1982) have concluded that such variables are among the most powerful predictors of psychological health. Measures of all five aspects of role were used in a study of white-collar workers by Bhalla et al. (1991). They were related to workers' reports of strain, job satisfaction and organisational commitment. The data suggested that overall role ambiguity, role conflict and role insufficiency were more strongly related to the outcome variables than were role overload or responsibility for other people.

Role Ambiguity

Role ambiguity occurs when a worker has inadequate information about his or her work role. As Warshaw (1979) has stated, "the individual just doesn't know how he or she fits into the organisation and is unsure of any rewards no matter how well he or she may perform." A wide range of events can create role ambiguity, many of them relating to novel situations and change (see Ivancevich & Matteson, 1980).

Role ambiguity manifests itself in a general confusion about appropriate objectives, a lack of clarity regarding expectations, and a general uncertainty about the scope and responsibilities of the job. Kahn et al. (1964) found that workers who suffered from role ambiguity were more likely to experience lower job satisfaction, a greater incidence of job-related tension, greater feelings of futility and lower levels of self-confidence. French & Caplan (1970) found that role ambiguity was related to a similar cluster of symptoms. They also showed that role ambiguity was related to increased blood pressure and higher pulse rates. Later research by Margolis et al. (1974) found a number of significant relationships between role ambiguity and symptoms of depression and low job motivation and intention to leave the job. Cooper and Marshall (1976) have pointed out that although the correlations reported in all these studies were significant and together paint a consistent picture, they were not particularly strong (only accounting for about 2-5% of the data variance). Furthermore, many of the measures of ill health were based on self-report (see section 4.2).

Role Conflict

Role conflict occurs when the individual is required to play a role which conflicts with their values, or when the various roles that they play are incompatible with one another. Kahn and his colleagues (1964) have shown that the greater role conflict in men, the lower job satisfaction and the greater job-related tension. French & Caplan (1970) found that mean heart rate was strongly related to perceived level of role conflict. It may also be related to increased risk of cardiovascular ill health (Ivancevich & Matteson, 1980). For example, Shirom et al. (1973), in a large study of Israeli men drawn from a range of occupations, found that there was a significant relationship between role conflict and incidence of coronary heart disease but only for white-collar workers. Cooper & Smith (1986) concluded that white-collar workers are more prone to role conflict than are manual workers.

Kahn et al. (1964) have suggested that those in 'boundary roles' (links between organisational levels or departments), such as foremen, are particularly prone to experience stress. Such roles have a high potential for conflict, and Margolis & Kroes (1974) found that foremen were seven times more likely to develop ulcers than shop floor workers.

Role Insufficiency

Role insufficiency refers to a failure of the organisation to make full use of the individual's abilities and training (for example, O'Brien, 1982). Such insufficiency has been reported to lead to feelings of stress (Brook, 1973) and is associated with psychological strain and low job satisfaction and organisational commitment (Bhalla et al., 1991).

Responsibility for People

Responsibility for people has been identified as a potential source of stress associated with role issues. Wardell *et al.* (1964) showed that responsibility for people, compared to responsibility for things, was likely to lead to greater risk of coronary heart disease. French & Caplan (1970) found that responsibility for people was significantly related to heavy smoking, raised diastolic blood pressure and elevated serum cholesterol levels. The literature on burn out (e.g., Leiter, 1991) also suggests that, in the caring professions at least, responsibility for people is associated with emotional exhaustion and the depersonalisation of relationships with patients. There is also evidence from the study of mental health referrals, by occupation, that those occupations involving continual contact with and responsibility for people are high risk (Colligan *et al.*, 1977).

Career Development

The lack of expected career development may be a source of stress, particularly in organisations which emphasise the relationship between career development and competence or worth. Marshall (1977) identified two major clusters of potential sources of stress in this area: first, lack of job security and obsolescence (fear of redundancy and forced early retirement); and, second, status incongruity (under or over promotion, and frustration at having reached the career ceiling). These have been related to adverse psychological effects as well as poor physical health (Kasl & Cobb, 1982; Margolis *et al.*, 1974) and are discussed below. These two sources of stress probably interact. Cooper (1978) has suggested that fear of obsolescence and failure resulting in demotion is likely to be strongest in those who believe they have reached their career ceiling, and that most will experience some erosion of status before they retire. Roberston & Cooper (1983) believe that these fears may give rise to stress if workers are unable to adapt their expectations to the reality of their situation. Not surprisingly, older workers are particularly vulnerable as they tend to place a high value on stability (Sleeper, 1975).

Job Insecurity and Poor Pay

Job insecurity and fear of redundancy can be major sources of anxiety, particularly if organisations expect, at the same time, commitment from their employees. The sense of inequity may exacerbate the experience of stress (Porter, 1990). Poor pay may be hazardous to health. While most workers will complain about levels of pay, the extremes of poor pay clearly have an effect on the worker's ability to remain healthy (Warr, 1992). Method or schedule of payment may also be a source of stress (for example, piece work) and may interact in its effects with the rate of working (Kasl, 1992).

Status Incongruity

The cost of status incongruity has been well researched in the United States. For example, Arthur & Gunderson (1965), in a study of naval personnel, claimed that promotional lag was significantly related to psychiatric illness. Interestingly, the literature on status incongruity also suggests a strong effect of non-work factors. For example, Kasl & Cobb (1967) concluded that stress related to parental status had 'strong long term effects on physical and mental health of adult offspring'. Shekelle *et al.* (1969) found that their sample of men in the United States whose present social class was substantially different from that of their childhood ran a significantly higher risk of coronary heart disease than men whose present social class was not.

Decision Latitude and Control

Decision latitude and control are important issues in job design and work organisation. They are often reflected in the extent to which employees can participate in decision-making affecting their work. However, there are other aspects to participation such as status which may also affect health and behaviour.

The experience of low control at work or of loss of control –low decision latitude– has been repeatedly associated with the experience of stress, and with anxiety, depression, apathy and exhaustion, low self esteem and increased incidence of cardiovascular symptoms (Terry & Jimmieson, 1999; Ganster & Fusilier, 1989; Sauter *et al.*, 1989; Karasek & Theorell, 1990). Interestingly, in a study of 244 occupations in Sweden, men consistently reported higher levels of control than women, even within female stereotyped jobs (Hall, 1991).

Following on from the work of Karasek, among others, it is often implied that increasing workers' control is universally beneficial. For example, Cox (1990) and Warr (1992) have argued that workers

should, ideally, be empowered to plan their work, and control their workloads, make decisions about how that work should be completed and how problems should be tackled. However, it has been argued by Neufeld & Paterson, (1989) that control can also be a double-edged sword: the demands implied by the choices involved in controlling situations can themselves be a source of stress.

Participation

Research suggests that where there are greater opportunities for participating in decision-making, greater satisfaction and higher feelings of self-esteem are reported (French & Caplan, 1970, 1972; Buck, 1972; Margolis *et al.* 1974; Spector, 1986). Non-participation appears related to work-related stress and overall poor physical health (Margolis & Kroes, 1974). French *et al.* (1982) have reported that lack of participation shows a strong relationship to job dissatisfaction but that this effect may be mediated by other variables relating to the overall person-environment fit.

Interpersonal Relationships at Work

It has been argued strongly that good relationships amongst workers and members of work groups are essential for both individual and organisational health (Cooper, 1981). A survey by the Ministry of Labour in Japan (1987) revealed that 52% of the women interviewed had experienced anxiety and stress, the main cause being unsatisfactory interpersonal relations at work (61%). Similarly, Jones *et al.* (1998) found that workers reporting high levels of stress and stress-related illnesses were 6½ times more likely to report "lack of support from people in charge at work" than the general working population.

Three important sets of relationships have been identified: relationships with superiors, relationships with subordinates and relationships with colleagues (Sauter *et al.*, 1992). Low interpersonal support at work has been found to be associated with high anxiety, emotional exhaustion, job tension and low job satisfaction and increased risk of cardiovascular disease (for example, Beehr & Newman, 1978; Davidson & Cooper, 1981; Pearse, 1977; Warr, 1992).

Social relationships both at work and outside the workplace are most commonly viewed as playing a moderating role, and adverse effects of exposure to other psychosocial hazards are more likely or more pronounced when relationships provide little support (Cobb & Kasl, 1977; Cohen & Willis, 1985; House & Wells, 1978). Karasek and colleagues (1982) in a study of over 1,000 male workers in Sweden, showed that support from supervisors and co-workers buffered the effects of job demands on depression and job satisfaction.

However, other research suggests a more direct effect of social support in offsetting the adverse effects of working conditions (Ganster *et al.*, 1986). In a recent meta-analytical study of 68 previous papers, Visweswaran *et al.* (1999) confirmed the presence of three general constructs (stressors, strains and social support). Their results indicated that social support had a threefold effect on work stressor-strain relations: it reduced the strains experienced,

mitigated perceived stressors, and moderated the stressor-strain relationship. Lobban *et al.* (1998) found that supervisory styles (in terms of providing direction and communicating with employees) may play a more dominant role in the stress process than is currently appreciated. They also suggest that supervisory relationships, either directly or mediated by other job characteristics, have significant additional influence on occupational stress that cannot be explained by the role or demand/latitude variables. Fielden & Peckar (1999) found that, although there is a direct link between the number of hours worked and stress levels, the number of hours worked was positively related to the perceived availability of social support.

Buck (1972) has reported that the 'considerate' behaviour of superiors appears to contribute inversely to workers' feelings of job pressure. Workers' participation in decision making results in them reporting greater job satisfaction and stronger feelings of self-esteem (Buck, 1972; French & Caplan, 1970, 1972; Margolis *et al.*, 1974). However, Donaldson & Gowler (1975) consider that pressure on managers to 'manage by participation' actually places them under increased pressure, and may cause feelings of resentment and anxiety. Robertson & Cooper (1983) discuss how competition at work, particularly among managers, may inhibit problem sharing and increase stress.

Violence at Work

There is growing literature on violence in the workplace (Cox & Leather, 1994; Beale *et al.*, 1998, Beale *et al.*, 1999; Leather *et al.*, 1998; Chappell & Di Martino, 1998; see also Standing & Nicolini, 1997, for a recent review) and on the related issue of post traumatic stress disorder (see Figley, 1985; Simon, 1999, for a review). There is strong evidence that exposure to violence in the workplace can cause damage to psychological as well as physical health[14] (Leather *et al.*, 1999). This is an area of increasing concern within the EU because, despite problems of definition across the different EU cultures, violence at work is a growing problem: 3 million workers reported being subjected to sexual harassment, 6 million to physical violence, and 12 million to intimidation and psychological violence (European Foundation, 1996). As a result of this concern, the European Commission (DG V) has published guidance on the prevention of violence at work (Wynne *et al.*, 1997).

Home-Work Interface

The concept of the work-home interface (or "work-home interference", WHI) relates not only to domestic life and the family but also to the broader domain of life outside of work. Most research has fo-

cused either on the relationship between managers and their spouses (Cooper, 1981) or on the use of leisure time (Gardell, 1973; Cox, 1980).

Work and Family

Hingley & Cooper (1986) have argued that problems relating to the interface between work and the family either involve resolving conflicts of demands on time and commitment, or revolve around issues of support. Much of the former literature focuses on women workers (see, for example, Davidson & Cooper, 1983) although commentary has been offered on men and particularly young managers (Weinberg *et al.*, 1999; Beattie *et al.*, 1974; Geurts *et al.*, 1999). The difficulties faced in resolving conflicts between work and family appear enhanced if the family has young children; again this may be particularly so for women workers (Larwood & Wood, 1979; Bhagat & Chassie, 1981). Early research suggested that most middle class wives appear to see their role, in relation to their husbands' job, as primarily 'supportive and domestic' (Pahl & Pahl, 1971). Some years later Cooper & Hingley (1985) found a similar pattern in the wives of their sample of executive men in the United Kingdom, although attitudes appeared to be changing. Failure to resolve adequately the conflicting demands between work and family may damage the support available from spouses, in particular, and the family in general.

Handy (1975) has explored the nature of a number of possible 'marriage-role' combinations in a study of executive managers. Consistent with other research, the most

---

[14] There are three main issues here: first, the accurate recording of data on violence at work and its aftermath so that an informed judgement can be made on the size of the problem; second, understanding the nature of such violence both from an individual and an organisational perspective; and third the development and evaluation of interventions designed to reduce the likelihood of violence occurring or reduce its impact on staff (Leather *et al.*, 1999). Recommendations on the management of violence at work have been published by a variety of bodies, including the British Health and Safety Executive (Mackay, 1987), the British Psychological Society (1992) and the Tavistock Institute of Human Relations (1986).

frequent combination was the "thrusting male–caring female", which was most beneficial to the working husband. Another increasingly common combination was what was effectively the dual career couple. In this combination, traditional role expectations appear to be challenged with the possibility of either or both partners experiencing feelings of threat and anxiety (Hingley & Cooper, 1986).

Wasted Leisure Time Syndrome

Spill-over effects from work might account for the possible wasting of constructive leisure time among some groups of employees (Gardell, 1973; Cox, 1980). The 'wasted leisure time syndrome' has been described by Gardell (1973) in terms of employees not finding time out of work to do more than potter about the home, skim through newspapers, watch television, and eat and sleep. Lundahl (1971) had observed in her Swedish study that those employed on heavy fatiguing jobs showed less involvement in leisure than those who were not. Both Gardell (1973) and Cox (1980) have suggested that more is involved than physical exertion, and the latter author has linked wasted leisure time to employees' psychological and behavioural adaptation to the demands of short cycle repetitive work. Wilensky (1960) has offered an explanation of the work-leisure relationship in terms of compensation, and this concept has also been used to account for the effects of repetitive work on the use of leisure time. Consistent with Wilensky's (1960) hypothesis, Strauss (1974) has suggested that employees can adjust to non-challenging work by lowering their expectations,

changing their need structure and making the most of social opportunities on and off the job. However, Kornhauser (1965) offered a similar explanation but with a more negative emphasis consistent with the hypotheses of Gardell (1973) and Cox (1980). He suggested that "the unsatisfactory mental health of working people consists in no small measure of their dwarfed desires and deadened initiative, reduction of their goals and restriction of their efforts to a point where life is relatively empty and only half meaningful".

Change

Change is often cited as a psychosocial hazard. However, it is not clear from the literature whether change *per se* is stressful or hazardous, or whether its possibly stressful nature is due to the uncertainty and lack of control which it often represents.

5.2.2 Content of Work

This section describes those psychosocial hazards which are related to the content of work and which are experienced as stressful and/or otherwise carry the potential for harm.

Task Design

There are several different aspects of job content which are hazardous: these include low value of work, the low use of skills, lack of task variety and repetitiveness in work, uncertainty, lack of opportunity to learn, high attentional demands, conflicting demands and insufficient resources (Kasl, 1992).

Semi-skilled and Unskilled Work

Such work is often characteristic of semi-skilled and unskilled jobs (Kornhauser, 1965; Caplan *et al.*, 1975; French *et al.*, 1982; Smith, 1981; Salvendy & Smith, 1981; Cox, 1985b). Cox (1985b) has reviewed the physical and psychological health effects of such work. Exposure to repetitive and monotonous work is often associated with the experience of boredom, and, in turn, with anxiety and depression, resentment, and generally poor psychological health (see: Kornhauser, 1965; Gardell, 1971; Laville & Teiger, 1976; Caplan *et al.*, 1975; Broadbent & Gath, 1981; O'Hanlon, 1981; Smith, 1981). For example, Kornhauser (1965) showed that among production workers in a car manufacturing plant in the United States, under-utilisation of skill was a particularly strong predictor of poor psychological health. There may also be an increased incidence of postural and musculo-skeletal problems, including work-related upper limb disorders (see, for example, Kuorinka, 1979; Chatterjee, 1987, 1992; Health & Safety Executive, 1990a), disorders of the digestive system (Laville & Teiger, 1976; Nerell, 1975) –although these disorders may be associated with shift working in such jobs (Rutenfranz, 1982)– and various changes in health-related behaviours, such as smoking and drinking (Ferguson, 1973). Exposure to noisy heavy repetitive work may also give rise to 'wasted leisure time syndrome' (Gardell, 1973; Cox, 1980) (see above).

Uncertainty

Uncertainty in work, in the form of lack of feedback on performance, is also a source of stress particularly when it extends across a long period of time (Warr, 1992). Such uncertainty may be expressed in ways other than lack of performance feedback, and may partly underpin the effects of other hazardous job characteristics; for example, uncertainty about desirable behaviours (role ambiguity) and uncertainty about future (job insecurity and redundancy).

Workload and Work Pace

Kornhauser (1965), from his study of Detroit car workers, suggested that "poor mental health was directly related to unpleasant working conditions, the necessity to work fast and to expend a lot of physical effort and to excessive and inconvenient hours". These various points, and others, are dealt with below.

Workload

Workload was one of the first aspects of work to receive attention (Stewart, 1976), and it has long been clear that both work overload and work underload can be problematic (Frankenhauser, 1975; Frankenhauser & Gardell, 1975; Lundberg & Forsman, 1979; Szabo *et al.*, 1983; Jones *et al.*, 1998). French and his colleagues, among others, have made a further distinction between *quantitative* and *qualitative* workload (French & Caplan, 1970; French *et al.*, 1974). Both have been associated with the experience of stress. Quantitative workload refers to the amount of work to be done while qualitative workload refers to the difficulty of that work. The two dimensions of workload are independent and it is possible to have work which involves quantitative overload and qualitative underload. Much short cycle repetitive assembly work is of this nature, and there is strong evidence that it offers a threat to both physical and psychological health (see above). Kahn & Byosiere (1990) have extended this line of argument by suggesting that workload is a function of quality, quantity and time.

Jones *et al.* (1998) found that workers reporting high levels of stress and stress-related illnesses were 4 $^1/_2$ times more likely to report problems with "working to deadlines" and "having too much work" than the general working population. Managers often cope with work overload by working longer hours (Uris, 1972), and although this may offer a short term solution to the immediate problem, long working hours –if sustained– may in themselves become problematic (see below).

Workpace and Time Urgency

Workload has to be considered in relation to work pace; that is the speed at which work has to be completed and the nature and control of the pacing requirement: self-, systems- or machine-paced. Within limits, control may be the decisive factor in determining health (Sauter *et al.*, 1989). There is strong evidence that machine- and systems-paced work, particularly if of high rate, is detrimental to both psychological and physical health (Bradley, 1989; Cox, 1985a, 1985b; Smith *et al.*, 1981; Smith, 1985). There is also evidence that electronic performance monitoring, for computer-based work, can produce a similar pattern of effects (see special edition of Applied Ergonomics, February, 1992).

Schriber & Gutek (1987) have identified a number of temporal dimensions that can be measured in organisational settings. Time urgency is usually treated as a property of the person (for example, in relation to type A behaviour) but it may well also be a property of the job. Johansson & Aronsson (1984) have suggested that VDT workers experience more time urgency in their work than do other occupational groups. Furthermore, Gael (1988) and Landy (1989), using task analysis, have demonstrated that differences in time demands of tasks can be readily identified with large and homogeneous samples of industrial workers.

Work Schedule

There are two main issues that relate to the effects of work scheduling on health: shift working and long work hours (see, for example, Canadian Mental Health Association, 1984). Work often involves both these factors (see, for example, Folkard & Monk, 1985; Work & Stress, 1989, special issue: 3).

Shift Work

Much of the literature relates to shift (and night) working and has been adequately reviewed elsewhere (see, for example, Boggild & Knutsson, 1999; Harrington, 1978; Johnson, 1981; Rutenfranz *et al.*, 1977, 1985; Monk & Tepas, 1985; Waterhouse *et al.*, 1992). Harrington (1978) concluded that "whereas good evidence exists to show that shift work, particularly night work, causes disruption of circadian rhythms and sleep patterns, the evidence for there being any major effect on health is slim." He did, however, also conclude that there may be a link between night work and digestive disorders, and between shift work in general and fatigue. He also commented that whatever effects did exist, they were likely to be greater in those who had difficulty in adapting to such forms of working or who had existing digestive or sleep related problems. Monk & Tepas (1985) reached broadly similar conclusions. In their recent study of night-shift nurses, Kobayashi *et al.* (1999) found that the cortisol and NK cell activity levels were low during the night shift, suggesting that night shift work is highly stressful and may prejudicial to biodefence.

Boggild & Knutsson (1999) reviewed 17 studies dealing with shift work and cardio-vascular disease risk. They suggest that methodological problems are present in most of these studies: selection bias, exposure classification, outcome classification, and the appropriateness of comparison groups. Boggild & Knutsson found that, on balance, shift workers were found to have a 40% increase in risk. Possible causal mechanisms of this risk via known cardio-vascular risk factors relate to circadian rhythms, disturbed sociotemporal patterns, social support, stress, health behaviours (smoking, diet, alcohol, exercise), and biochemical changes (cholesterol, triglycerides, etc). They conclude that the risk is probably multifactorial, and that the literature has focused on the behaviour of shift workers, thus neglecting other possible causal connections.

Long Work Hours

The European Community Directive on Working Time, which should have been implemented in Member States of the European Community by November 1996, contains several requirements related to working hours, including the right of employees to refuse to work more than 48 hours a week. Much of the research in this area has focused on the problems of shift-working, emphasising this aspect of working hours. However, there is much less information about the effects of overtime work, which is a central element of the terms of the Directive. Research to date has been restricted to a limited range of health outcomes –namely, mental health and cardiovascular disorders (Spurgeon *et al.*, 1997). Other potential effects which are normally associated with stress (for example, gastrointestinal disorders, musculoskeletal disorders, and problems associated with depression of the immune system) have received little attention. There have also been few systematic investigations of performance effects, and little consideration of the implications for occupational exposure limits of extensions to the working day. Existing data relate largely to situations where working hours exceed 50 a week and there is a lack of information on hours below this level, which is of direct relevance to European Union legislation.

In their review, Spurgeon *et al.* (1997) conclude that the attitudes and motivation of the people concerned, the job requirements, and other aspects of the organisational and cultural climate are likely to influence the level and nature of health and performance outcomes. However, they also suggest that there is currently sufficient evidence to raise concerns about the risks to health and safety of long work-ing hours. Long hours of work, from ex-tended work days of 12 hours (see, for example, Rosa et al., 1989) to sustained working over several days with sleep loss (see, for example, Stampi, 1989; Patton et al., 1989; von Restorff et al., 1989), has been shown to increase fatigue. Much of the evidence, especially in the later area, has come from studies on military work and performance.

The European Foundation's (1996) Work-ing Conditions Report indicated that a high proportion of workers across the EU work long hours[15] (49% work more than 40 hours per week, and 23% more than 45 hours). The data also revealed that health problems (stress and back ache) in-creased with the hours worked. Com-pressed work weeks, with 12-hour working days, have been associated with feelings of increased fatigue (Rosa & Colli-gan, 1986). Rosa et al. (1989) have shown that after seven months adaptation to a 3-4 day /12 hour rotating shift schedule there were reductions in sleep and decre-ments in subjective alertness compared to previous work on a 5-7 day / 8 hour sched-ule. The increases in self-reported stress which also occurred were attenuated by the shortened work week.

Sustained working can cause or be other-wise associated with sleep loss and per-ceived exertion or fatigue (for example, Ryman et al., 1989). Performance can be severely compromised by accumulation of sleep debt (Stampi, 1989). The upper limit of human performance for working inten-sively and continuously is 2-3 days (Haslam, 1982; Naitoh et al., 1983). Per-formance effects can be detected in vigi-lance tasks and those involving cognitive and verbal performance (Angus & Hesle-grave, 1983; Haslam, 1982). Physical per-formance, particularly if of moderate intensity appears more resistant to impair-ment (for example, Patton et al., 1989).

Some occupational groups, such as junior doctors, are cause for special concern. For example, Spurgeon & Harrington (1989) have reviewed the effects of long working hours on the performance and health of junior hospital doctors. In the United King-dom, particular work rotas meant that un-til recently junior doctors were working spells of around 102 hours. Spurgeon & Harrington (1989) concluded that a num-ber of studies have shown that a signifi-cant proportion of newly qualified doctors develop some degree of psychological ill health. They argue that this may be related to sleep loss which probably increases doc-tors' vulnerability to other work hazards. The establishment of a Task Force has brought about significant reductions in the numbers of hours worked by junior doc-tors, but Fielden & Peckar (1999) still found that direct link between the number of hours worked and stress levels (al-though the number of hours worked was positively related to the perceived availabil-ity of social support). Junior hospital doc-tors used social support as a coping strategy significantly more often than se-nior hospital doctors, with both perceiving the hospital environment as a more effec-tive source of social support than the home environment. Despite having access

---

[15] Defined as more than 40 hours per week.

to higher levels of effective social support, junior hospital doctors faced significantly greater sources of stress and poorer mental health than their senior counterparts.

There is an association between long hours of work and death from coronary heart disease Breslow & Buell (1960) found that individuals under 45 years of age who worked more than 48 hours a week had twice the risk of death from coronary heart disease than similar individuals who worked 40 or fewer hours per week. Another study of young coronary patients revealed that one in four had been working at two jobs and an additional two in five had been working more than 60 hours a week (Russek & Zohman, 1958).

Control over work schedules is an important factor in job design and work organisation. Such control may be offered by flexitime arrangements (Landy, 1989). It is interesting to note that although the introduction of flexitime arrangements may be associated with little change in behaviour (Ronen, 1981), they nonetheless can have a positive effect on workers (Narayanan & Nath, 1982; Orpen, 1981). In this case it is likely that it is the *perceived* control offered by such arrangements rather than the actual exercise of control that is important (Landy, 1992). Lack of control over work schedules may represent a source of stress to workers.

5.2.3 New hazards: "The changing world of work"

Large scale socio-economic and technological changes in recent years have affected workplaces considerably. They are often collectively referred to as "the changing world of work". This term encompasses a wide range of new patterns of work organisation at a variety of levels: teleworking and increased use of information and communication technology (ICT) in the workplace; downsizing, outsourcing, subcontracting and globalisation, with the associated change in employment patterns; demands for workers' flexibility both in terms of number and function or skills; an increasing proportion of the population working in the service sector, and a growing number of older workers; self-regulated work and teamwork, etc. The research corpus is still developing in these areas (e.g., see Rosenstock, 1997, on NIOSH's ongoing research project on downsizing), but there is some preliminary evidence that even changes which may be thought to *enhance* the work environment can produce the opposite effect. For example, Windel (1996) studied the introduction of self-regulating team work in the office of an electronics manufacturer. Although self-regulated work may be a source of increased self-efficacy and offer enhanced social support, Windel found that after 1 year work demands had increased and well-being decreased when compared to baseline data. The data suggested that the increase in social support brought about by self-regulating teams was not sufficient to counteract increased demands caused by the combination of a reduction in the number of staff and increases in managerial duties. Meta-analytical studies have also shown either mixed consequences (Bettenhausen, 1991; Windel & Zimolong, 1997) or higher rates of absenteeism and staff turnover (Cohen and Ledford, 1994) as a result of the implementation of team work or self-regulated work.

It is clear that changes which have such a profound impact on the way organisations operate may carry associated potential hazards that need to be monitored for their impact on health and well-being.

5.3

ANIMAL STUDIES

Generally, the literature on animal behaviour has not been incorporated into this Report. However, such studies have also suggested the characteristics which define stressful situations for many different species (Turkkan et al., 1982). Most relate to acute and well-defined stressors in the workplace. These include: the interval between aversive events, the availability of warning signals, the availability of avoidance or escape contingencies, changes in established procedures, and the duration of exposure to the aversive event and its severity. While the importance of these characteristics has been established through studies on animal behaviour, mostly within a conditioning paradigm, they do have face validity in relation to the workplace, and some map easily onto the characteristics listed in Table 1.

There appear to be critical temporal dimensions involved with most aversive

tasks largely defining the interval between aversive events, and such intervals are not always the shortest possible. They vary with task and outcome (see, for example, Brady (1958) and Rice (1963) for the effects of avoidance schedule timing on ulceration in laboratory animals). Van Raaij et al. (1996) studied the effects of a low-intensity chronic intermittent unpredictable noise regimen on various parameters of immune function. Male wistar rats were exposed to a randomised noise protocol (white noise, 85 dB, 2-20 kHz) for 10 hours per day, 15 minutes per hour over a total period of 3 weeks. Control animals were exposed to ambient sound only. Immune function was monitored after 24 hours, 7 days, and 21 days of noise exposure. Noise induced several significant changes in immune function in a time-dependent differential pattern involving both immunosuppression and immunoenhancement. Their results show that various parameters of immune function are affected differentially over time in a period of chronic mild noise stress, possibly due to sequential activation of different physiological mechanisms.

The availability of a warning signal appears to attenuate the physiological response to an aversive event (for example, Weiss, 1972; Miller et al., 1978) as do the availability of avoidance or escape contingencies (for example, Anisman et al., 1980; Sklar & Anisman, 1981). Changing established or learnt procedures produces extensive endocrinological changes (for example, Brady, 1975). Short exposures to aversive stimuli may not have cumulative effects, and animals appear to adapt to long exposures. Medium range durations of exposure may therefore be most effective in producing physiological responses to aversive stimulation (for example, Forsyth & Harris, 1970). Generally, the greater the intensity of the aversive event, the stronger the physiological and pathological responses (Turkkan *et al.*, 1982), although this is not always the case (see, for example, Ulrich & Azrin, 1962).

5.4

DISTRIBUTION OF PSYCHOSOCIAL WORK HAZARDS

There is little good evidence relating to the distribution of psychosocial hazards across different types and levels of work and across different countries. There have been few, if any, surveys which provide an adequate comparison of a wide range of different types and levels of work (European Foundation, 1996).

A survey in the early 1990s attempted to map the physical and organisational constraints of work[16] in the [then] twelve member states of the European Community and in former East Germany (European Survey on the Work Environment 1991-1992). Briefly, organisational problems affected a higher proportion of workers than did physical problems. The main organisa-

tional problem areas were 'lack of influence over one's work' (35-40%), 'involvement in short cycle repetitive work' (about 25%) and 'long working hours'. 16% of men and 7% of women reported working over 50 hours per week. The findings from more recent studies are broadly similar (European Foundation, 1996, 1997).

Broad comparisons can be drawn between, say, manual and managerial work. Warr (1992) has suggested that much manual work tends to be associated with extremes of workload (overload or underload), low levels of decision-making and participation, and low task variety. Where the work is deemed to be semi-skilled or unskilled, there is also the problem of low use of skill or skill potential. Managerial work, in stark contrast, is more often associated with work overload, role related problems and uncertainty. French *et al.* (1982) have provided some support for this suggestion. In their survey in the United States, manual workers reported having low job complexity and low requirement for concentration (and an underutilisation of their skills), low participation and low support. Professional workers, by comparison, reported having high job complexity and no under utilisation of their skills, and good participation and support.

The ongoing series of Whitehall studies (e.g., Marmot & Madge, 1987; Stansfeld *et al.*, 1995; Bosma & Marmot, 1997; Stansfeld *et al.*, 1999), offer data which compare the work characteristics of men of different grades in the Civil Service in the United Kingdom. The work of the lower grades has been characterised by under

---

[16] The organisational constraints referred to in the European Survey on the Work Environment 1991-1992 are equivalent to the psychosocial hazards referred to in this report.

use of skills and by low social contact with others at work. To a somewhat lesser extent, it also involves low control and lack of task variety. Interestingly, within this particular organisational context, the work of the higher grades is also characterised by low social contact and under use of skills but to a lesser extent. The most obvious differences between lower and higher grades relate to former's lack of control and variety in work.

Our knowledge of how the distribution of psychosocial hazards relates to occupational risk is somewhat complicated by suggestions that it is particular synergistic combinations of such hazards that carry the greatest threat to health (Levi, 1984). Evidence of such synergy is claimed from the work of Karasek, but –as discussed in section 3.2.2– the evidence for such a synergistic effect is weak. Another example is provided by Martin & Wall (1989), who have described a case study where the introduction of computer-based technology into the workplace resulted a high level of stress reflecting the *combination* of increased cost responsibility with increased attentional demands.

5.5

SUMMARY

It is possible from the available literature to explore the effects of the more tangible hazards of work on the experience of stress and on health, and to identify those psychosocial hazards which pose a threat to employees. Most literature reviews have identified the need for further research and development to translate this information into a form which can be used in the auditing and analysis of workplaces and organisations. Such a model, together with practical implementation strategies, has been provided by Cox *et al.* (2000) and is described in more detail in section 7.2.

RESEARCH

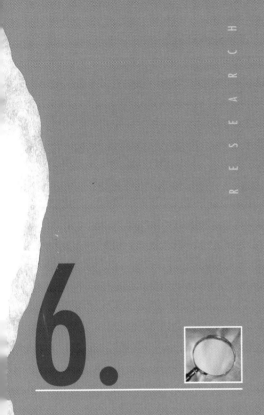

6.

STRESS AND HEALTH

Over the past two decades, there has been an increasing belief that the experience of stress necessarily has undesirable consequences for health. It has become a common assumption, if not a "cultural truism" (Leventhal & Tomarken, 1987), that it is associated with the impairment of health. Despite this, the evidence is that the experience of stress does not *necessarily* have pathological sequelae. Many of the person's responses to that experience, both psychological and physiological, are comfortably within the body's normal homeostatic limits and, while taxing the psychophysiological mechanisms involved, need not cause any lasting disturbance or damage. However, it is also obvious that the negative emotional experiences which are associated with the experience of stress detract both from the general quality of life and from the person's sense of well-being. Thus the experience of stress, while necessarily reducing that sense of well-being, does not inevitably contribute to the development of physical or psychological disorder. For some, however, the experience may influence pathogenesis: stress may affect health. At the same time, however, a state of ill health can both act as a significant source of stress, and may also sensitise the person to other sources of stress by reducing their ability to cope. Within these limits, the common assumption of a relationship between the experience of stress and poor health appears justified (Cox, 1988a).

This section presents a brief overview of the broad range of health and health-related effects which have been variously associated with the experience of stress. More detailed discussions are available elsewhere (for example, Cox, 1978; Kristensen, 1996; Cincirpini *et al.*, 1984; Stainbrook & Green, 1983; Millar, 1984, 1990). It focuses on changes in health and health-related behaviours and physiological function, which together may account for any linkage between that experience and psychological and physical health (Cox *et al.*, 1983).

This Report also refers to the concept of *organisational healthiness*. This concept (see Cox & Thomson, 2000) is based on an analogy with individual health and is a derivation of sociotechnical systems thinking. It concerns the nature and viability of organisations as systems, and includes measures of the perceived quality of the social organisation and its relationships with the technical organisation. The term 'the health of the organisation' can be thought of as referring to its condition, in the same sense that the parallel term 'the health of the individual' refers to the general condition of the person. In itself introducing the notion of the 'condition' of the organisation is intellectually insufficient, and further refinements need to be made: the health of the individual is often defined in terms of their condition of body, mind and spirit (Longman's Dictionary of the English Language, 1992). In parallel terms, it has been suggested by Smewing & Cox (1996) that the health of the organisation is "the general condition of its structure and function, management systems and culture." This may be re-phrased as the *quality* of its structure and function, management systems and culture. Additionally, a distinction needs to be made between what is healthy and what is not, in terms of 'general condition'. Healthy individuals, and healthy organisations, are those which are seemingly sound, that is fit-for-purpose, thriving and able to adapt in the longer term. Expanding on this, a healthy organisation is "an organisation in which the different components, which define its general condition, sum to it being 'fit-for-purpose', thriving and adaptable, and which is perceived positively by its employees." This is the definition adopted for this Report.

6.1

It is convenient to summarise the possible health and health-related effects of stress under two headings: psychological and social effects, and physiological and physical effects.

EFFECTS OF STRESS: AN OVERVIEW

The experience of stress can alter the way the person feels, thinks and behaves, and can also produce changes in their physiological function (Stansfeld et al., 1999; Sauter & Murphy, 1995; Cincirpini et al.., 1984; Stainbrook & Green, 1983). Many of these changes simply represent, in themselves, a modest dysfunction and possibly some associated discomfort. Many are easily reversible although still damaging to the quality of life at the time. However, for some workers and under some circumstances, they might translate into poor performance at work, into other psychological and social problems and into poor physical health (e.g., Devereux et al., 1999). Nevertheless, the overall strength of the relationship between the experience of stress and its antecedents on one hand and health on the other is consistent but moderate (Baker, 1985; Kasl, 1980a, 1984).

6.2

PSYCHOLOGICAL AND SOCIAL EFFECTS

The psychological effects of stress may be expressed in a variety of different ways, and involve changes in cognitive-perceptual function, emotion and behaviour. Some of these changes may represent attempts to cope, including changes in health-related behaviours. There is evidence that some health-promoting behaviours, such as exercise and relaxation, sleep and good dietary habits, are impaired by the experience of stress, while other health-risk behaviours, such as smoking and drinking, are enhanced. Other behaviours, such as sexual behaviour, which may be health-neutral, can also be impaired and that impairment become a secondary cause of stress. Similarly, increases in health-risk behaviours can also become secondary causes of stress if sustained. Particular reference may be made to psychological dependency on alcohol or smoking. Social behaviour, and interper-

sonal relations, may be impaired by the experience of stress, possibly reflecting more fundamental psychological changes in, for example, irritability, attention span and memory. Stress-related impairments of social relations may both create secondary problems and reduce the availability of social support.

Interestingly, the literature which describes the translation from a normal psychological reaction to events to *psychological* illness is not well formed, except in the case of post traumatic stress and related disorders (see, for example, Figley, 1985; Hillas & Cox, 1987). A variety of psychological sequelae have been related to exposure to extremely threatening situations such as catastrophes and disasters (Logue, 1980; Logue *et al.*, 1981), war (Blank, 1981; Milgram, 1982) and terrorism (Bastiaans, 1982).

Psychological ill health has also been associated with work stress (e.g., Stansfeld *et al.*, 1999). One of the classical studies in this area is that by Colligan *et al.* (1977). They conducted a survey, by occupation, of all first admissions to 22 of the 27 community mental health centres in Tennessee (USA), from January 1972 through June 1974. 8,450 cases were considered from 130 different occupational groups. Occupations were ranked according to estimated admission rate per 1000 workers and by z scores. Z scores were calculated for observed against expected frequencies of admission on the basis of the relative frequency of members of the groups in the population. These rates were then compared and the top 30 ranks reported. The group with by far the highest rate was health technology technicians, and five others in the top 30 were relatively low status health care occupations. Many of the occupations which were represented in the top 30 also involved continual inter-action with others (patients, clients, customers, etc.), including human service occupations. It has been argued that the presence of so many health care occupations in the top 30 is an artefact and simply reflects their better knowledge of psychological health issues and of appropriate health care facilities. However, this criticism cannot be so readily applied to the personal service groups represented in the survey. Operatives ranked 28th (out of 130).

6.3

PHYSIOLOGICAL AND
PHYSICAL EFFECTS

Contemporary research into physiological and physical health correlates of stress began in the 1920s and 1930s with the work of Cannon (1929, 1931) and Selye (1936). Since then much has been published in this area (e.g., Landsbergis et al., 1995; Meijman et al., 1995; Kawakami & Haratani, 1999).

A large body of data has been accumulated concerning physiological responses in people exposed to stressors in laboratories. Adrenaline and cortisol have become known as *stress hormones* because, in men, levels of both hormones consistently rise in response to stress in laboratory-based investigations. If chronically repeated, elevation of adrenaline and cortisol is likely to have long-term consequences for health, especially cardiovascular health, partly via the effects of the hormones on blood pressure and serum cholesterol lev-

els (Pollard, 1997). Research on people conducting their everyday lives, both in and out of work, is necessary to establish whether the same responses are shown on a day to day basis. Such research requires new methodologies and careful data collection. So far, it has been shown that adrenaline and blood pressure do seem to vary in expected ways. Other responses in everyday life, including those of cholesterol, cortisol and the immune system, are less well characterised.

6.3.1 Mechanisms of Stress-related Physiopathology

Zegans (1982) has suggested that there are three different ways in which the physiological changes associated with the experience of stress occur: as a concomitant physiological response to an appraisal of threat or a failure of coping; as a physiological response to an appraisal of threat when active coping is not possible; and, as a non-specific response during the initial orientation-alarm state. Zegans (1982) has also suggested a number of ways in which such physiological responses might contribute to pathology. The acute response may itself cause damage, particularly if an already compromised organ system is involved. If this is not the case, then repeated occurrence of that insult might cause more permanent damage. The experience of stress and the physiological insult it causes might become chronic and again cause more permanent damage. Together these three cover the often cited conditions for increased wear and tear on the body (Selye, 1950): exposure to stressors which is severe, frequent or of long duration. However, Zegans (1982) has also argued that there are other mechanisms which might contribute to the translation of a normal transient physiological response into one of pathological significance. Most appear to relate to the interaction between stress responses and other physiological systems, particularly control systems. First, the experience of stress might result in an inappropriately severe response because either a deficiency in relevant control systems or the stress response might stimulate other less benign reactions, again because of the lack of control elsewhere.

Zegans (1982) has also argued that the potentially pathogenic effects of the stress response express themselves by challenging the various body systems which integrate and defend physiological function, and which underpin its link with behaviour. These systems include the hypothalamic-pituitary-adrenal cortical axis, the autonomic nervous system-adrenal medullary axis, the immune system, the reticular activating system, and the cognitive-affective centres of the brain (Zegans, 1982). Much attention, in the past, has been focused on the role of the adrenal glands in stress physiology and there are several reviews available (for example, Selye, 1950; Levi, 1972; Cox & Cox, 1985; Szabo et al., 1983). Stress can cause endocrine hypoactivity and hyperactivity (Lipton, 1976) and alter the balance of autonomic control altering function in the cardiovascular, respiratory, secretory and visceral systems (Lisander, 1979). It appears to impair or distort the immune response (Stein et al., 1981; Kawakami & Haratani, 1999). It can

distort visceral perception (Brener, 1978), alter sleep patterns with knock-on effects on a variety of other activities (Weitzman et al., 1975), and induce changes in other behaviours, some of which have significance for health (Antelman & Caggiula, 1977).

There have been a small number of studies that have exposed subjects to stressful situations and measured a wide range of physiological, largely biochemical, responses and subsequently factor analysed these data. Given that such studies require much control and resources, it is often difficult to capture sufficient data (by case) to satisfy the requirements of factor analytic procedures (see, for example, Ferguson & Cox, 1993). However, these studies are of interest, and those that have been reported have similar findings. Rose et al. (1967) analysed circulating hormone levels in 46 men undergoing basic military training. They found five factors: a cortisol factor, a catecholamine factor, two factors related to androgens and oestrogen, and one related to thyroid function. A study of 115 military trainees by Ellertsen et al. (1978) identified three factors: a cortisol factor, a catecholamine factor and a testosterone-free fatty acid factor. Ryman & Ursin (1979) studied 31 American Navy company commanders in stressful conditions and again reported a factor model of their physiological responses consistent with that reported by Ellertsen et al. (1978). Ursin (1979) has suggested that these three physiological response factors might be differentially related to pathology. Subjects who respond with a predominant cortisol response might be more prone, according to the model of Henry & Stephens (1977), to depression, disorders of the immune system and gastric or duodenal ulcers. Using the same argument, Ursin (1979) linked catecholamine responders to cardiovascular problems and possibly renal conditions.

Turkkan et al., (1982) have reviewed the available evidence from animal studies and have come to a conclusion not inconsistent with that expressed by Zegans (1982). From the animal evidence, there appear to be four physiological systems which are particularly vulnerable to stress. The four are: the cardiovascular system (Brady & Harris, 1977; Schneiderman, 1978; Kristensen, 1996 for a recent review); endocrine system (for example, Mason, 1968; Stone, 1975); gastro-intestinal function (see Turkkan et al., 1982) and immune system (for example, Monjan, 1981; Kawakami & Haratani, 1999). Stress-related dysfunction in these systems is potentially significant for physical health.

Given this consensus, it is not surprising that the literature on stress and physical health largely focuses on a number of particular conditions, although a large number of others are commonly cited as being, to some extent, stress-related (see, for example, Cox, 1978; Millar, 1984). It has been suggested (Cox, 1978) that, under certain circumstances, *all* physical conditions are potentially susceptible to stress effects. If this is true, then questions must be asked about which are the more susceptible or the most directly susceptible, and how that susceptibility is affected by the nature of work and the workplace. The more susceptible conditions appear to be

those relating to the cardiovascular and respiratory systems (for example, coronary heart disease and asthma: Marmot & Theorell, 1988; Kristensen, 1996, Bosma & Marmot, 1997; Stansfeld et al., 1995, 1999), the immune system (for example, rheumatoid arthritis and possibly some forms of cancer), and the gastro-intestinal system (for example, gastric and peptic ulcers), and those relating to the endocrine, autonomic and muscular systems. Among this group, most attention is currently being focused on the immune system (e.g., Peters et al., 1999; Borella et al., 1999; Kawakami & Haratani, 1999). There are several reviews available concerning the general relationship between stress, emotion and immune function (for example, O'Leary, 1990) but few, if any, overviews of the effects of work-related stress on that function.

6.4

WORK-RELATED
PSYCHOIMMUNOLOGY

There are a number of studies, many of them Norwegian, which demonstrate a link between the experience of work stress and changes in immune system activity, both cellular and humoral. Vaernes et al. (1991) have reported a study of Norwegian air force personnel in which they showed significant correlations between perceived work stress and immunoglobulin levels, and also complaints related to immune system activity. Levels of complement component C3 (humoral immunity) appeared particularly sensitive to variations in perceived work stress, and 31% of the variance in this measure could be accounted for by three work stress items relating to: taking the job home, having to lead other people, and problems with subordinates. Interestingly, levels of IgM and IgG (cellular) did not correlate in any substantial way with the work stress measures. There was weak evidence of a linkage between IgA (cellular) and

some aspects of perceived work stress. The immunological measures correlated with the measures of health complaints related to immune system activity.

Endresen et al. (1991) have reported a somewhat similar study of Norwegian bank workers. Their data suggested that T-cell number (not examined in the Vaernes et al. (1991) study) and C3 (both cellular), and also IgM (humoral), were sensitive to both perceived work stress and associated emotional distress. There are a number of other studies from the Norwegians which support the finding of a linkage between the experience of work stress and immune system activity. These include studies on: offshore divers (Bergan et al., 1987), submarine officers (Vaernes et al., 1987), nurses (Endresen et al., 1987; Arnestad & Aanestad, 1985), primary school teachers (Ursin et al., 1984) and shift workers in the processing industry (Vaernes et al., 1988). While it may be safe to conclude that such a linkage exists, particularly in relation to cellular mechanisms, the direction of this relationship is not yet clear (the data are correlational) nor is its significance for health. Animal studies do, however, suggest that environmental stimuli (stressors) can alter the effectiveness of the immune system and reduce, in some circumstances, its ability to defend against both external infective agents and tumour growth (e.g., Van Raaij et al., 1996). Much of this evidence has been usefully summarised in reviews of the role of psychosocial factors and psychophysiological processes in cancer(s) (Ader, 1981; Fox, 1981; Sklar & Anisman, 1981; Cox & Mackay, 1982; Irwin & Anisman, 1984; Cox, 1984).

6.4.1 Mechanisms

Work by Riley (1981) provides one possible account of the way the experience of (work) stress may influence the development of cancers. Riley (1981) has argued that stress-associated pathologies will not be observed, despite the presence of stress, if there is no disease process already in existence. He is arguing here for a role for stress in the development of existing cancers rather than in the aetiology of new cancers. Second, even if there is an existing latent pathology, the effects of stress will not be observed unless the disease is under the control of the immune system. This may account for stress effects on the development of some cancers and not others. Third, the effects of stress will only be observed if there is some functional balance between the individual's defences and the developing cancer. Where one or other is obviously dominant, any additional effects of stress may be impossible to detect. This means that the effects of stress may not be detectable in the early and terminal stages of cancer development. This model was largely developed from Riley's studies on rodents to account for cancer development (see Riley, 1979, 1981; Riley et al., 1981) but might be usefully applied to other diseases which involve the immune system activity (see, for example, Cox, 1988b).

6.4.2 Other Pathologies

A considerable variety of different pathologies, both psychological and physical, have been associated with the experience of stress through work (Holt, 1982). Those disorders usually cited as being stress-relat-ed include: bronchitis, coronary heart disease, mental illness, thyroid disorders, skin diseases, certain types of rheumatoid arthritis, obesity, tuberculosis, headaches and migraine, peptic ulcers and ulcerative colitis, and diabetes (Cox, 1978; Cooper and Marshall, 1976; Kroes, 1976, Selye, 1976; Bosma & Marmot, 1997; Stansfeld et al., 1995, 1999; Kristensen, 1996).

According to Selye (1956) repeated, intense or prolonged elicitation of this physiological response, it has been suggested, increases the wear and tear on the body, and contributes to what he has called the 'diseases of adaptation'. This apparently paradoxical term arises from the contrast between the immediate and short-term advantages bestowed by physiological response to stress (energy mobilisation for an active behavioural response) to the long-term disadvantages (increased risk of certain 'stress-related' diseases).

Furthermore, the general occurrence of physical ill-health has also been related to the experience of stress. For example, Nowack (1991) has reported on the relationship between perceived stress and coping style, on the one hand, and self-reported ill health, on the other. The frequency and severity of physical ill health (Wyler et al., 1968) were measured. After controlling for demographic variables and for psychological well-being, perceived stress was shown to be a strong predictor of both the frequency and severity of physical ill health. About 30% of the variance in the latter was accounted for by perceived stress. However, there is the problem of the direction of effect given that the study was correlational in nature, as many in this area are.

Attention focused, in earlier years, on peptic ulcers as the prototypical work stress disease (Holt, 1982). However, despite this attention, opinion is divided on whether or not the condition is stress related. In 1967, Susser concluded, from a review of the literature, that there is a link, while somewhat later Weiner (1977) stated that no such link had yet been proved. However, at the same time, House et al. (1979) reported a link between work stress –particularly stressful relations with others– and ulcers, after controlling for seven possibly confounding variables.

Much attention has also been focused on cardiovascular diseases, especially coronary heart disease. The origin of coronary heart disease, like many chronic degenerative conditions, is multifactorial but work factors and stress have clearly been indicated (see, for example, Poppius et al., 1999; Kristensen, 1996; Cooper & Marshall, 1976; House, 1974; Jenkins et al., 1976). However, the evidence is not completely unequivocal and negative findings have been reported (see, for example, Haynes et al., 1978a, 1978b). One well-established and frequently replicated finding is the link between type A behaviour pattern and cardiovascular disease (see, for example, Jenkins et al., 1968).

There has been evidence for a long time that the experience of stress can contribute to an acceleration of the disease process in at least one particular type of rheumatoid arthritis (see Genest, 1983, 1989). Rimon & Laakso (1985) have sug-

gested that there are two separate types of rheumatoid arthritis: one, a disease form less connected with genetic factors and potentially more influenced by stress, and a second form more associated with heredity disposition and less influenced by psychosocial processes. These groups may overlap with those described by Crown et al. (1975). These authors distinguished between patients on the basis of the presence or absence of rheumatoid factor (RF). The sero-positive group, with RF, showed a more negative psychopathological profile than those without RF. Such findings have been replicated by other workers such as Gardiner (1980) and Volhardt et al. (1982).

6.5

ORGANISATIONAL EFFECTS

not be personally or professionally accept-able: people may continue to turn up for work under stress but perform poorly: pre-senteeism[17].

If significant numbers of workers are expe-riencing and expressing the effects of stress at work, then the problem assumes organisational proportions. There has been some (unsupported) suggestion that if (about) 40% of workers in any group (department or organisation) are facing stress related problems, then that group or organisation can also be said to be un-healthy in some way. From the literature, there appear to be several effects of stress which may be of more direct concern to organisations. The most frequently cited appear to be: reduced availability for work involving high turnover, absenteeism and poor time keeping (all essentially 'escape' strategies), impaired work performance and productivity, an increase in client com-plaints (cf: Jones et al., 1988) and an in-crease in employee compensation claims (Barth, 1990; Lippe, 1990; Neary et al., 1992). For some, escapist strategies may

---

[17] Presenteeism is a term used to refer to "being phys-ically present at work but mentally absent" (e.g., Cooper et al., 1996). It is contrasted with absenteeism.

6.6

SUMMARY

There is evidence that the experience of stress at work is associated with changes in behaviour and physiological function, both of which may be detrimental to employees' health. Much is known about the possible mechanisms underpinning such effects, and particular attention has been paid to pathologies possibly associated with impaired immune activity as well as those more traditionally linked to stress, such as ulcers, coronary heart disease and rheumatoid arthritis.

RESEARCH

7.

THE ASSESSMENT AND MANAGEMENT OF WORK-RELATED STRESS

The European Agency's Topic Centre on Good Practice – Stress at Work (TC/GP-ST) collects and evaluates existing good practice information about stress at work across the EU and beyond. Consequently, the present Report will not examine actual practice, but –having reviewed the research into the nature, causes and effects of work-related stress in the preceding sections– will deal briefly with the research evidence regarding the assessment and management of stress at work.

7.1

THE ASSESSMENT OF WORK-RELATED STRESS: THE CONTROL CYCLE

As discussed earlier, there are numerous reviews of research into psychosocial hazards and stress (e.g., Cox, 1993; Cartwright & Cooper, 1996; Borg, 1990; Hiebert & Farber, 1984; Kasl, 1990; Cooper & Marshall, 1976), and a large number of papers dealing with stressors in almost every conceivable work setting and occupation. However, as Cox (1993) indicates, "research into the nature and effects of a hazard is not the same as assessment of the associated risk". Indeed, most published studies would provide very little data that could be used for a risk assessment. Many "stress surveys" tend to identify only hazards or only outcomes, whereas the object of a risk assessment is to establish an *association* between hazards and health outcomes, and to evaluate the risk to health from exposure to a hazard.

An almost unavoidable corollary of the paucity of adequate risk assessments is that most "stress management" interventions target the individual rather than the organisation (the former is usually seen as cheaper and less cumbersome: see section 7.5), are often *off-the-shelf* designs, and are entirely divorced from the process of diagnosis of the problems -if diagnosis takes place at all (Cox, 1993). A different type of approach is therefore required in order to carry out risk assessments which can then inform the design of interventions -in other words, a strategy that actually *asks the question* before giving the answer. Such a strategy has already been suggested for the control of physical hazards (e.g., Council Directive 89/391/EEC ["Framework Directive"]; European Commission, 1996): the *control cycle*, which has been defined as "the systematic process by which hazards are identified, risks analysed and managed, and workers protected" (Cox & Griffiths, 1995) and comprises 6 steps:

1. Identification of hazards
2. Assessment of associated risks
3. Implementation of appropriate control strategies
4. Monitoring of effectiveness of control strategies
5. Re-assessment of risk
6. Review of information needs, and training needs of employees exposed to hazards

Steps 1 through 5 are recursive and designed to ensure continuous improvement of occupational health and safety at work. Each step can be conceptualised as a further cycle of activities similar to a goal-seeking process as described by Schott (1992). As a systematic and comprehensive approach to assessing the risks within the work environment, the control cycle satisfies current legal requirements. However, it is still necessary to evaluate whether it represents a scientifically valid and reliable strategy to assess psychosocial hazards.

Occupational health psychology borrowed the concept of risk assessment from the field of physical hazard control (Cox & Cox, 1993). The formalised approach required by EU legislation on physical hazards (e.g., Council Directive 98/24/EC) is ideally implemented through a problem-solving approach such as the control cycle. For example, the EC guidance document clearly subscribes to the notion of the control cycle as the favoured approach in its definition of risk assessment: "a systematic examination of all aspects of the work undertaken to consider what could cause injury or harm, whether the hazards could be eliminated, and if not what preventive or protective measures are, or should be, in place to control the risks" (European Commission, 1996 § 3.1). The risk assessment approach also has in its favour the advantage of being an already familiar strategy with employers. It also provides an integrated framework which could ostensibly accommodate psychosocial hazards as an additional category of hazards to be found in the workplace.

However, considerable difficulties emerge when trying to broaden the risk assessment approach to include psychosocial hazards: The first task is to achieve a definition of the terms used in risk assessment. This is far from straight-forward and has often proved difficult even in the more

tangible area of physical hazards[18]. A review of the literature suggests that there is reasonable consensus on the definitions of the basic terminology. For example, the EU Member States have agreed on "accepted and practical" definitions for the following fundamental terms:

Hazard: The intrinsic property or ability of something (e.g. work materials, equipment, work methods and practices) with the potential to cause harm.

Risk: The likelihood that the potential for harm will be attained under the conditions of use and/or exposure, and the possible extent of the harm.

(European Commission, 1996, § 1.2)

Although these are acceptable at a basic level and as a guideline for employers, from a scientific perspective there is a danger of stretching the parallel too far when the need arises to operationalise those definitions. For instance, there remain some doubts as to whether the above definition of "hazard" would include some characteristics of the work environment such as "broad corporate policies: paid leaves of absence, promotion, health insurance coverage, etc." (Landy *et al.*, 1994). Moreover, it is not possible to establish an exact conceptual or practical symmetry between physical and psychosocial hazards. Exposure to certain levels of radiation is known

---

[18] See, for example, the Internet-based project sponsored by the Organization for Economic Cooperation and Development to harmonise the definitions of the basic generic terms involved in the risk assessment of chemical hazards (Organization for Economic Cooperation and Development, 1997)

to be an indisputable risk to *every* worker's health, while one can be very confident that other substances are safe for *everyone*. However, it is not obvious that such statements can be put forward with any confidence for most –if not all– psychosocial hazards. Could *anything* within the work environment be a potential psychosocial hazard? If so, the definition of hazard could become meaningless. If not, what aspects of work could never be hazardous, and why? Similarly, whereas psychosocial hazards can be conceptualised as *part* of a continuum that is represented by "psychosocial hazard" at one end and "salutogenic factor" at the other (e.g. from *very low* to *very high job control*), physical hazards such as asbestos would seem to be negative *per se* and lacking a potential salutogenic role (even its absence would not be health-enhancing but merely neutral).

A study by Kang *et al.* (1999) in the physical hazards field illustrates these conceptual and practical differences between physical and psychosocial hazards. They examined the usefulness of an *automatic hazard analyser* (AHA). This system performs hazard analysis in terms of both functional failure and variable deviation in the search for possible causes of accidents. The result of analysis provides a pathway leading to an accident, and, therefore, gives not only clear understanding of the accident, but useful information for hazard assessment. Kang *et al.* applied AHA to the feed section of an olefin dimerization plant, and the system performed better than traditional qualitative hazard analysis methods. Research into the assessment of

psychosocial hazards is clearly in too early a stage to permit the use of an expert system such as that described by Kang *et al.*

With regard to "harm", in order to categorise "the extent of harm" referred to in the definition of risk, the EC guidance document suggests the following range of outcomes:

Minor damage
Non-injury accident
Minor injury (bruise, laceration)
Serious injury (fracture, amputation, chronic ill-health)
Fatal
Multiple-fatality

(European Commission, 1996§ 4.8.3)

It would not be a simple task to achieve a consensus on a hierarchy of "degrees of psychological harm" similar to that which is easily available for physical harm. Moreover, a number of studies (Landy *et al.*, 1994; Kasl, 1987, 1990; Johnson, 1996) have identified the difficulties encountered when researchers and practitioners have to decide on what indicators of both physical and psychological well-being they should use: "In a scenario which repeated itself over and over, a particular approach was seen as pretty reasonable for surveillance of injuries, somewhat useful for a narrow band of work-related diseases, but inadequate for the intended broader spectrum of such diseases, and by implication inestimably useless for surveillance of psychological disorders" (Landy *et al.*, 1994).

It is clearly not merely a matter of agreeing on what the appropriate indices are (individual health or organisational functioning? Both? Why? Should the selected indices take into account the culture of the organisation and / or occupational group, or should the culture itself be an index of organisational healthiness?). It is arguably *more* difficult to find reliable and valid sources of information for the indices: Psychiatric diagnoses, treatment and care-seeking records, symptom checklists, indices of functional effectiveness, "positive mental health" measures, indicators of "quality of life", health-related behaviours, employers' and trade unions' records (where they exist at all), data on use of occupational health services, and data on compensation and litigation are all either seriously or fatally flawed due to self-selection, recording and reporting problems, complex operationalisation, or confounding variables. To be fair, these difficulties also arise for the assessment of physical hazards (e.g. inaccurate organisational records, unwillingness of companies or individuals to report accidents or "near-misses" which may reveal possible deficiencies in their control systems, etc.), However, the problems for psychosocial hazards are compounded by the difficulties intrinsic to monitoring outcomes which are less perceptually obvious than physical injuries or fatalities.

This elusive nature of psychosocial hazards also contributes to making causal relationships between hazard and harm considerably more difficult to establish (Johnson & Hall, 1996). One only needs to consider the differential effort required to prove beyond doubt the effects of asbestos or radiation on individual health and those of most of the psychosocial hazards men-

tioned earlier (e.g. the vast literature accumulated on the effects of job control on cardiovascular disease; see section 6.3).

Finally, much of the difficulty in drawing a scientifically valid and exact parallel with the risk assessment of physical hazards lies in the problems encountered by researchers when trying to measure the work environment. These were examined in detail in section 4.

To summarise, the risk assessment model is very helpful as an analogy and represents a useful strategy for the assessment of psychosocial hazards at work. However, there are a number of issues to bear in mind: (a) the operationalisation of definitions of hazard, (b) the identification of adequate indices of harm that can also be reliably monitored, (c) satisfactory proof of a causal relationship, and (d) problems of measurement of the work environment.

7.2

A RISK MANAGEMENT APPROACH TO WORK-RELATED STRESS

Cox et al. (2000) have described a framework that takes into consideration the problems outlined in the previous section and aims to overcome the difficulties of adapting the control cycle to the assessment and reduction of psychosocial hazards. At the heart of the risk management described by Cox et al. (2000) are two distinct but intimately related cycles of activity: risk assessment and risk reduction. These form the basic building blocks for the staged model of risk management. However, in addition to risk assessment and risk management, three other components are specified. These include "evaluation" and "organisational learning and training". The model also introduces a new linking stage between risk assessment and risk reduction, that of "the translation process". Because all aspects of the risk management process should be evaluated, and not just the outcomes of the risk reduction stage, the "evaluation" stage is treated as all encompassing and supra-ordinate to the other stages. This model of risk management is shown below (Figure 4). The risk reduction stage, in practice, tends to involve not only prevention but also actions more orientated towards individual health and welfare.

Figure 4: A framework model of risk management for work stress

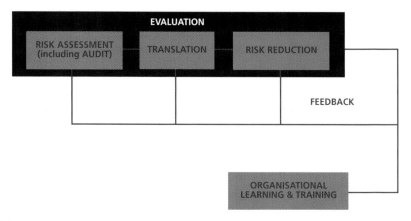

There are parallels between this model and the organisational intervention process being developed by applied researchers in the USA. The "interventions team" working as part of NORA (National Institute, 1999) also emphasise the need for evaluation and the feedback of evaluation data to inform earlier stages in the overall analysis-intervention cycle (Goldenhar et al., 1998) (see Figure 5 below).

Figure 5: Intervention research in occupational safety and health: A conceptual model (from Goldenhar et al., 1998)

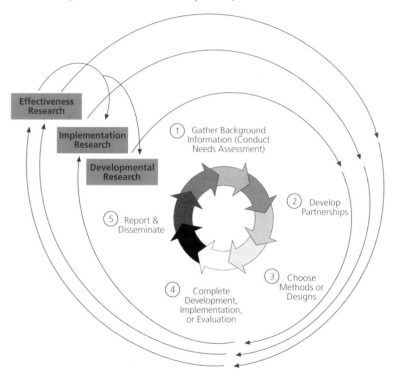

Cox et al. (2000) have also described a five-step strategy to carry out a risk assessment process in practice. The different phases are summarised in Figure 6 below.

Figure 6: The five steps for risk assessment for work stress

The five steps for the risk assessment for work stress:

• Step 1: Familiarisation
• Step 2: Work Analysis Interviews
• Step 3: Assessment Survey
• Step 4: Audit of Existing Management Control and Employee Support Systems
• Step 5: Analysis and Interpretation of Assessment Data

Each step builds on information collected during any preceding step. The initial steps (Steps 1, and 2) are designed to build a model of the work and working conditions of the assessment group that is good enough to support the design and later use of the assessment instrument (Step 3). This instrument is used to quantify the workers' exposure (at group level) to all the significant stressors associated with their work and working conditions, and assess their health.

The five steps are largely sequential with one possible exception. The Audit of Existing Management Control and Employee Support Systems (step 4) can be conducted either in parallel with the Work Analysis Interviews, or following the Analysis and Interpretation of Assessment Data. It is often most convenient to conduct it in parallel with the Work Analysis Interviews. In this case, the information collected can usefully contribute to the working model of the assessment group's situation that is built up in the early stages of the assessment. Finally, all information is analysed and interpreted (step 5).

These five steps can be mapped onto an overall assessment strategy as shown in Figure 7 below.

Figure 7: Risk assessment strategy and procedures

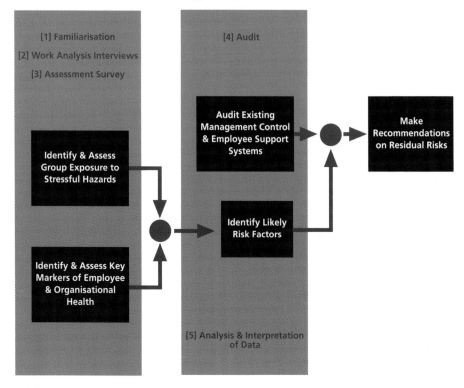

7.3

THE MANAGEMENT OF
WORK-RELATED STRESS

cursory consideration to risk management in Section 5 under the heading "Actions as a result of risk assessment at work". Although useful as a tool for organisations undertaking a risk assessment, the document –as would be expected given its purpose– only offers a generic flowchart of options to choose from depending on the results of the assessment. Furthermore, the lack of examination of the effectiveness of stress management programmes remains one of the main shortcomings in the scientific literature (van der Hek & Plomp, 1997).

The scientific literature on risk management is even more sparse than that on risk assessment. Exhaustive literature reviews have failed to produce more than a handful of studies (e.g. Jackson, 1983; Israel *et al.*, 1996). Apart from reviews of stress management interventions (e.g., van der Hek & Plomp, 1997; Dollard & Winefield, 1996; Burke, 1993; International Labour Organization, 1992; Murphy, 1984 & 1988; Cox, 1993), much of what is published is limited to prescriptions and recommendations (e.g., Briner, 1997; Kompier *et al.*, 1998), guidance for what amounts to "good management practice" with some psychological content (e.g., International Federation, 1992, and various publications by NIOSH in the USA) or generic standard *recipes* for a healthier work environment (e.g. Landy, 1992; Locke, 1976). The EC's 1996 *Guidance on Risk Assessment at Work* document gives

7.4

PRINCIPLES OF STRESS

MANAGEMENT

In one of the early papers in this area, Newman and Beehr (1979) suggested that stress management can be classified in terms of its objectives and strategies, its focus or target, and the agent through which it is carried out. This section examines each in turn.

7.4.1 Objectives

While only a minority of organisations appear to be directly and deliberately addressing the management of occupational stress, those actions which are being taken can be classified in terms of their implied objectives. There are, at least, three distinct sets of objectives which have been adopted by organisations in managing work stress and its health effects (Cox *et al.*, 1990; Dollard & Winefield, 1998):

1. *Prevention*, often control of hazards and exposure to hazards by design and worker training to reduce the likelihood of those workers experiencing stress.

2. *Timely reaction*, often based on management and group problem-solving, to improve the organisation's (or managers') ability to recognise and deal with problems as they arise.

3. *Rehabilitation*, often involving offering enhanced support (including counselling) to help workers cope with and recover from problems which exist.

Within this model, many authors make a distinction between those objectives which concern or focus on the *organisation* (organisational stress management) and those that concern and focus on the *individual* (personal stress management) (for example, De Frank & Cooper, 1987; Ivancevich & Matteson, 1986; Ivancevich *et al.*, 1990; Keita & Sauter, 1992; Matteson & Ivancevich, 1987; Murphy, 1984, 1988; Murphy & Hurrell, 1987; Newman & Beehr, 1979; Quick & Quick, 1984; Quick *et al.*, 1992a; Schwartz, 1980).

While equal attention is now being paid to both in the literature (and in legislation), much practice is biased towards the personal (and more clinical) approach. At the same time, while attention is being paid to preventive and rehabilitative strategies, less attention is being focused on reactive strategies. One exception is that of Cox & Cox (1992) who describe a 'stress tool kit' for line and specialist managers to help them recognise and deal with employees' problems which are stress-related.

7.4.2 Agency and Target

Given that a clear distinction is made between the different possible objectives, Cox *et al.* (1990) have suggested that the issues of agency and focus or target, as raised by Newman and Beehr (1979), can be paired and effectively dealt with in terms of three questions:

- Organisation as agent and target: what can the organisation do to put its own house in order?
- Organisation as agent and workers as target: what can the organisation do to enhance the support it offers workers?
- Employee as agent and target: what can individual workers do better to manage their work and any associated experience of stress?

It was pointed out by Cox *et al.* (1990) that the second and third questions overlap. In reality, they question whether the organisation can help the individual to help themselves. This is often the explicit goal of employee support programmes. Logically, there is a fourth pairing (worker as agent and organisation as target) which describes the involvement of workers in organisational development.

7.5

COMMON INTERVENTIONS:
THEIR EFFECTIVENESS

To summarise, there are three common types of intervention to be found in the literature on stress management (see, for example, Murphy, 1988; Cooper & Cartwright, 1997; Dollard & Winefield, 1996; Kompier et al., 1998):

1. Primary: some form of organisational or work development which attempts to reduce stressors (control hazards), including work design and ergonomics (e.g., Jones et al., 1988; Golembiewski et al., 1987)

2. Secondary: worker training either in the form of health promotion or psychological skills (e.g., Lindquist & Cooper, 1999)

3. Tertiary: employee assistance (largely focused on the provision of counselling).

These are described more fully below. However, despite a burgeoning literature

on the subject, the relative effectiveness of such programmes has been difficult to determine, largely because of methodological deficiencies inherent in much of the relevant research and lack of adequate evaluations (e.g. Briner, 1997; van der Hek & Plomp (1997); see also section 7.1). Murphy et al. (1992), Kompier et al. (1998) and van der Hek & Plomp (1997), for example, consider that evaluations should include cost-benefit analyses and assessments of employee satisfaction, job stressors, performance, absenteeism and health status. However, they rarely do so. Van der Hek & Plomp (1997) found that, out of 342 scientific papers on stress management interventions, only 37 referred to some kind of evaluation research, of which 7 were 'evaluated' on the basis of anecdotal comments from participants.

Beehr & O'Hara (1987), Burke (1993), Dollard & Winefield (1996) have reviewed the difficulties involved in the design and evaluation of stress management interventions. Most designs are either 'pre-experimental' or 'quasi-experimental' (true experiments being difficult to conduct in organisations) and vary considerably in their ability to control for the various 'threats' to validity. For example, in the study of the effects of counselling on employees' anxiety levels, anxiety scores may appear to return to normal over repeated testing but, if employees were initially selected (or volunteered) on the basis of extreme scores, this may simply reflect a regression to the mean. Since most secondary and tertiary stress management programmes are voluntary, selection effects may operate: the characteristics of participants and non-participants may be quite different. Selection effects have been discussed in detail in the evaluation of employee fitness programmes (see, for example, Jex, 1991).

One of the advantages of stressor reduction interventions is that they attempt to change stressors common to all, thereby side-stepping selection effects (Burke, 1993). Further, many studies claim to show improvements as a result of interventions that may in fact be due to non-specific effects such as treatment credibility, expectations or even just sitting quietly. On the rare occasions that control groups have been included in occupational stress interventions, it is not uncommon for both treatment and control groups to show improvements. Similarly, where different types of stress management programmes have been compared it is not unusual for all to produce similar improvements (for example, Hart, 1987). These reservations and others have been echoed in publications by Keita & Sauter (1992) and Quick et al. (1992b). With the paucity of sound data on the outcomes of such interventions, it is not surprising that it has been very difficult to make judgements concerning the cost benefits (the merits of an intervention in financial terms) or cost effectiveness (merits in comparison with available alternatives). This issue is also referred to later in this section when dealing with employee assistance programmes.

Many reviews (Murphy, 1988; Ivancevich et al., 1990; Burke, 1993; Dollard & Winefield, 1996; Cooper & Williams, 1997) find most stress management interventions are individually focused, designed for man-agerial and white-collar workers and concerned with changing the worker as opposed to work or the work environment. For example, Williamson (1994) found that out of 24 evaluative studies of stress interventions being conducted at the time, 21 focused on the individual, (e.g., stress management programmes, relaxation, etc.) and only 3 focused on change at the organisational level. Kompier et al. (1998) offer four main reasons why interventions that target the individual appear to be more numerous in the scientific literature: "the opinions and interests of company management, the nature of psychology, the difficulty of conducting methodologically 'sound' intervention studies and the denominational segregation of stress research". Briner (1997) has also noted that "primary" interventions are the least popular, and has suggested that "in an organizational context [...] changing the nature of the job or the organization may be considered more daunting and complex than simply buying-in some of the other types of interventions".

This may be a reflection of the nature and influence of management views in some countries. Surveys in the United States among management and union groups have revealed clear differences in their views of stress (for example, Singer et al., 1986). Whilst management emphasise individual (secondary and tertiary) interventions, seeing personality, family problems or lifestyle as being prominent sources of stress, union groups consider social and organisational factors such as job design and management style as being both more responsible and more suitable targets for intervention. Dollard & Winefield (1996) suggested that "the politics involved in conceptualizing the stress problem and in recognizing psychological disorder as a leading occupational health issue in Australia has impaired advances towards its prevention and treatment and the status of occupational stress as a national policy issue". It has been suggested that in Scandinavia, where responsibility for working conditions is shared equally between labour and management groups, organisational approaches to stress management are generally more common than elsewhere (Landsbergis, 1988). The dominance of management views, particularly in the United States, has contributed to the development of Employee Assistance Programmes and Stress Management Training ahead of stressor reduction / hazard control techniques.

Stressor Reduction (Hazard Control) Interventions

Murphy (1988) identified and reviewed several interventions which addressed the nature and design of the work environment or organisation (Jackson, 1983; Wall & Clegg, 1981; Pierce & Newstrom, 1983). His interpretation of these studies was framed by the concept of control in relation to stress and health (see Averill, 1973; Miller, 1979; Thompson, 1981; Cox & Ferguson, 1991). The issue of control is a pervasive one throughout the stress literature.

The study by Wall & Clegg (1981) manipulated worker control over significant aspects of the work process; the manipulation in the Jackson (1983) study produced modest increases in worker con-

trol; the manipulation in the study by Pierce & Newstrom (1983) –introduction of flexitime systems– could also be said to increase worker control over some aspects of their work. All three studies demonstrated the effectiveness of the control related manipulations in reducing workers' report of stressors and aspects of their experience of stress.

Jackson (1983) reported a well-designed evaluation of an intervention study conducted amongst staff working in 25 outpatient clinics in hospitals in the United Kingdom and designed to reduce role ambiguity and conflict. The hypothesis under test was that increased participation in decision-making would decrease the experience of role problems. Clinic supervisors were given appropriate training on participation and the number of staff meetings held in the clinics was increased. The effects of these interventions were evaluated against a number of outcome measures using a Solomon 4 group design. Significant reductions in role ambiguity and role conflict were observed in the intervention clinics after 6 months follow up.

A study by Jones et al. (1988), which focused on the number of malpractice complaints received by a medical practice, produced positive results. Four studies were conducted to examine both the relation between stress and medical malpractice and the impact of stress management programs in reducing malpractice risk. 76 hospitals and more than 12,000 individuals participated. In study 1, hospital departments with a current record of malpractice reported higher levels of on-the-job stress than did matched low risk departments. In study 2, workplace stress levels of 61 hospitals correlated significantly with frequency of malpractice claims. In study 3, a longitudinal investigation was conducted to evaluate the impact of an organisation-wide stress management programme on the frequency of reported medication errors. Results suggested a significant drop in average monthly medication errors as a result of the program. Study 4 was a 2-year longitudinal investigation that compared the frequency of medical malpractice claims. Twenty-two hospitals that implemented an organisation-wide stress management programme had significantly fewer claims compared with a matched sample that did not participate.

MacLennan (1992) presents several problem situations facing institutions in the US and details some of the organisational remedies instituted to tackle them. Although these interventions were not evaluated, they provide useful examples of the type of approach considered promising. The First American Bankcorp of Nashville, Tennessee (which has 150 banks) experienced problems with high turnover, sickness absence and low productivity. They formed 'action teams' from each area of operation who were trained in problem identification and problem-solving. Employees rotated on and off the teams with the result that many people had the opportunity to participate. In the first year, turnover was cut from 50% to 25%. MacLennan details several interventions undertaken by other US banking institutions designed to reduce work-family conflicts including onsite day centres for pre-school and school children, maternity

leave arrangements, job protection schemes, arrangements for part-time work for returning mothers and fathers, flexitime and working at home, the provision of 'family sick days' and unpaid leave to be used for children, spouses or elderly parents. Other organisational interventions (MacLennan, 1992) concerned sexual harassment and work flow problems in government and stressors facing long distance lorry drivers, air traffic controllers and AMTRAK (railway) engineers. In the latter case, for example, management had reduced the number of engineers driving fast trains from two to one, with no consideration given to the fact that most of the drivers had been used to working in pairs for some time, nor that the seating and instrumentation in cabs may have needed alteration. Following complaints of increased levels of stress, the union hired consultants to identify the relevant stressors facing solitary drivers of high-speed trains, many of which could be tackled by organisational interventions.

Murphy & Hurrell (1987) describe the development of a worker-management 'stress reduction committee', as a possible first step in any stress management intervention. In their study, the results of a stress management workshop provided the information required for an employee survey. The committee then reviewed and prioritised the identified sources of stress, planned organisational interventions designed to address them and presented them to management, recommending an annual audit. Such approaches acknowledge the importance of the process as well as the content of interventions by the involvement of employees.

Golembiewski *et al.* (1987) describe an intervention in which a programme of organisational development was implemented. The programme affected all the members of the organisation and took place over 13 months. The authors measured levels of burnout, job involvement and turnover rates. They found that the level of burnout decreased (and remained low for at least four months), and decreased somewhat in the following nine months. There were also improvements in the rates of turnover, which persisted after the initial implementation of the programme.

Finally, Landsbergis and Vivona-Vaughan (1997) carried out, and evaluated, an intervention based on organisational development, action research and Karasek's (1979) job strain model. In this study, employee committees conducted problem diagnosis, action planning and action taking in two departments in a public agency over a period of one year (there were also two waiting-list control departments). Pre- and post-intervention measures were obtained from workers in all four departments via a standardised survey instrument, and qualitative information was also obtained at a four-month follow-up by telephone interviews with members of the problem-solving committees.

The results obtained by the evaluation survey were mixed: for members in Intervention Department 1, values at post-test were nearly all in a more negative direction than at pre-test. However, for Intervention Department 2 all study variables were in a more positive direction. The feedback from the evaluation questionnaire was also

somewhat critical: 52% (Department 1) and 39% (Department 2) of staff members who did not participate in the committees felt that the intervention had been either "ineffective" or only "slightly effective". Nevertheless, over two-thirds of them felt that the programme should be initiated in other departments. The follow-up interviews revealed a possible explanation for this pattern of results: a divisional reorganisation begun by the agency one week before post-test had affected all 4 departments and resulted in feelings of frustration and disappointment. Workers feared that the reorganisation would result in the loss of the gains achieved by the problem-solving committees. As a result, in Department 1 many of the proposed changes (e.g., a policy and procedures manual and an associated committee) had not been completed. The authors discuss the reasons for the mixed results both in terms of the methodological limitations and the inevitable constraints of applied research.

Stress Management Training

In 1984, Murphy reviewed thirteen published and unpublished studies on personal stress management for NIOSH. Although the programmes varied considerably in terms of the work groups involved, the nature of the techniques and the outcome measures used, Murphy (1984) was able to make several general observations on those programmes and their effectiveness.

The majority of the programmes focused on training in techniques such as relaxation and other behavioural skills, meditation, biofeedback, and cognitive restructuring. All the studies reviewed involved some form of relaxation training, and in all but one case (Peterson, 1981) in combination with cognitive or behavioural skills training. This generally consisted of a mixture of several different techniques including assertiveness and personal effectiveness training, cognitive restructuring and the reshaping of personal perceptions by logical reasoning. All techniques seemed to involve, to some degree, strengthening the person's self esteem or sense of personal worth. Of the 32 outcome measures used in the thirteen studies, 27 clearly related to the individual and only 3 to the organisation.

Murphy (1984) concluded that a number of significant benefits accrued to individuals, including reductions in physiological arousal levels, in tension and anxiety, in sleep disturbances and in somatic complaints. A number of workers also reported an increased ability to cope with work and home problems following completion of their programme. Not all of these effects were maintained at follow up testing which was usually between 3-9 months later.

Many of these studies are solely reliant on self-report measures and there has been a relative paucity of more objective data in evaluation studies. A study by Ganster et al. (1982) employed both self-report measures of psychological and somatic complaints and measures of adrenaline and noradrenaline levels. In that study, a stress management training program was evaluated in a field experiment with 79 public agency employees who were randomly assigned to treatment (n = 40) and control (n = 39) groups. The training program con-

sisted of 16 hours of group exposure distributed over 8 weeks. Using procedures based on those developed by Meichenbaum (1977), treatment subjects were taught to recognise and alter their cognitive interpretations to stressful events at work. Subjects were also taught progressive relaxation techniques to supplement this process. Dependent variables were adrenaline and noradrenaline excretion at work, anxiety, depression, irritation and somatic complaints, all measured three times (pre-test, post-test and 4 months after treatment). Treatment subjects exhibited significantly lower adrenaline and depression levels than did controls at the post-test, and 4 month follow up levels did not regress to pre-test levels. However, treatment effects were not replicated in a subsequent intervention on the original control group. The authors did not recommend the general adoption of such stress management training programmes.

Murphy (1984) also listed a number of advantages to adopting personal stress management programmes, beyond those for individual participants:
1. They can be established and evaluated quickly without major disruption to work routines.
2. They can be tailored to individual workers' needs and also contribute to the control of non-work problems.
3. They can link into worker assistance programmes (counselling).

He concluded that the *major* disadvantage of such programmes is that they are not designed to reduce or eliminate sources of stress at work but only to teach workers more effective coping strategies. A number of likely reasons for the imbalance between the number of individual- and organisation-focused stress prevention programmes carried out have been outlined earlier.

The cost-benefit considerations of personal stress management programmes were not directly addressed by Murphy in 1984, although he did point out the delivery costs of the various techniques considered. He concluded that biofeedback was probably the most expensive while meditation was probably the least expensive. A cost-benefit ratio has been attempted for such techniques by Manuso (cited in Schwartz, 1980). He calculated that every dollar spent on personal stress management programmes might realise $5.52 in benefits for the organisation as a result of decreased symptom activity and increased performance.

Employee Assistance Programmes

Employee Assistance Programmes (EAPs), whose origins can be seen in organisations' concerns over to the cost of alcoholism in the workplace, have flourished in the United States and Europe. In their narrower form, such programmes focus on 'picking up the pieces' (with counselling and helplines) for the 'troubled employee', addressing drug abuse, personal crises, and marital and family problems. Some are broader, embracing concerns such as impending retirement and relocation. In effect, the range of benefits that could be offered is infinite. The service may be provided in-house, by consortia or by specialist EAP contractors.

For example, Cooper et al. (1992a, 1992b) have described the evaluation of a pilot scheme for individual based stress counselling in the United Kingdom Post Office. The evaluation was based on a simple pre-/post-test design which compared the psychological health and absence behaviour of those using the scheme with a broadly matched control group of non-participants. Measures of job satisfaction and organisational commitment were also taken. While the authors recognised weaknesses in the design, the data suggested that counselling was effective in improving self-reported psychological health and absence from work, but not job satisfaction and organisational commitment.

Murphy et al. (1992) point out that the provision and management of such programmes is not as straightforward as it may appear at first sight: there is a delicate balance between assisting individuals and protecting and promoting the interests of organisations. Berridge & Cooper (1993) refer to this as an "uneasy alliance" where "the balance of interests may well only be maintained because of the lack of fundamental analysis of either group's function and activities on the part of the other". As far as stress management is concerned, data from an EAP (with individuals' anonymity guaranteed) could be a useful source of information, enabling an organisation to identify 'high stress' departments or procedures (Murphy et al., 1992) and perhaps to plan organisational interventions.

There has been much interest in the legal implications of EAP provision in the United States. Whilst some commentators view

EAPs as a reflection of a general 'helping' trend in labour relations, and some question how far EAP provision would have progressed without compensation legislation and the union movement (Berridge & Cooper, 1993), others suggest that EAPs represent a "legal expedient of providing employees with a chance, so that the employer who follows EAP to the letter meets arbitration criteria when firing becomes inevitable" for problem employees (Nobile, 1991). Some have argued that EAP provision may actually *increase* an organisation's legal liability by, for example, opening itself up to accusations of incorrect assessment of a problem, of inadequately trained or qualified service providers or of unequal access.

Although such programmes have been limited by methodological difficulties and by issues of confidentiality, there have been claims for considerable financial advantages. In the United States, the GM programme, which assists some 100,000 employees each year, has been said to save the company $37 million per year (Feldman, 1991). A study by the Paul Revere Life Insurance Company claims to show a saving of $4.23 for every dollar spent (Intindola, 1991). Reviewing this area, Berridge and Cooper (1993) point out that there has been much criticism of the basis of such claims and much argument as to the most appropriate method of evaluation: cost-benefit analysis, cost effectiveness analysis, utility analysis, peer review, employee attitude surveys or statistical case sampling. "In all such evaluation the independence of the evaluator needs to be combined with the maintenance of confidentiality and the integrity of programme data. The reconciliation of these requirements, along with the demands of management, renders the evaluation of EAPs extremely problematic and open to criticism from all concerned" (Berridge and Cooper, 1993).

One component of broadly based EAPs is often stress management training. However, such interventions are usually offered without any link in to counselling or other forms of employee assistance.

7.6

SUMMARY

Many existing off-the-shelf "stress" surveys fail to provide a sufficiently detailed basis for sound intervention programmes. This section has considered the advantages and difficulties in extending existing risk management paradigms from the field of physical hazards to cover psychosocial hazards. Recent studies in the EU and the USA have described an assessment and intervention framework which takes into consideration the problems identified in previous section of this Report and aims to overcome the difficulties of adapting a control cycle approach to the management of work-related stress. This framework also includes aspects of organisational learning and training which may bring additional benefits to organisations. Stress management programmes have been classified according to some basic principles of intervention: objective (prevention, timely reaction, or rehabilita-

tion), agency (organisation and/or employees) and target (organisation and/or individuals). The scientific literature suggests that organisational-level interventions (or, at least, intervention programmes that target the organisation *as well as* the individual employees) may be the most beneficial for both individuals and organisations. It is also frequently argued that stress management interventions should be evaluated. This is essential for the proper development of the area. However, a review of the stress management literature reveals that most interventions are weak, targeting only the individual, and that very few are adequately designed or evaluated in scientific terms. This section has discussed some of the reasons for this disparity between scientific requirements and actual practice. Finally, the three types of interventions (primary, secondary and tertiary) have been evaluated here in terms of their effectiveness. The available evidence –described in detail– suggests that, although few in number, organisational-level interventions that aim to eliminate or control the hazards within the work environment have significant advantages and represent the best way forward.

RESEARCH

8.

CONCLUSIONS

This section attempts to summarise the findings of the present Report and identify areas in need of further research.

8.1

vidual, but others relate to the design and management of work and interventions to improve the work environment.

DEFINING STRESS

There is a growing consensus on the definition of stress as a negative psychological state with cognitive and emotional components, and on its effects on the health of both individual employees and their organisations. Furthermore, there are now theories of stress which can be used to relate the experience and effects of work stress to exposure to work hazards and to the harmful effects on individual and organisational health that such exposure might cause. Applying such theories to the understanding of stress at work allows an approach to the management of work stress through the application of the notion of the control cycle. Such an approach has proved effective elsewhere in health and safety. It offers a systematic problem-solving system for continuous improvement in relation to work stress. There are several distinct areas in which more research is required: some relate to the individual, but others relate to the design and

8.2

INDIVIDUAL DIFFERENCES:
WORK ABILITY AND COPING

paradigm for individual differences may not be capable of providing the necessary progress. Could, for example, the concept of coping be replaced in the literature by, say, that of control? Is all coping an attempt to establish perceived control within one or more domains of experience –cognition, emotion, physiology or behaviour? What are the effects of ontological variables such as ageing on coping and the experience of stress?

The experience of stress is partly dependent on the individual's ability to cope with the demands placed on them by their work, and on the way in which they subsequently cope with those demands, and related issues of control and support. More information is required on the nature, structure and effectiveness of individuals' abilities to meet work demands and to cope with any subsequent stress. The need for more information on coping is widely recognised (see, for example, Dewe, 2000), but relatively less attention has been paid to the need better to understand this concept in relation to those of work ability and competence, although this is being flagged in relation to ageing research (e.g., Griffiths, 1999a; Ilmarinen & Rantanen, 1999).

It is suggested here that a more radical approach is required, as the present research

8.3

MEASURING STRESS

ing argued for throughout is better measurement procedures, conforming to recognised good practice in relevant areas, and applied within a declared theoretical context.

More research and development are required in relation to the measurement of the experience of stress and related emotion and the overall stress process. The inadequacy of single one-off measures is widely recognised in the literature but, despite this, they continue to be used, and across studies focused on different aspects of the stress process. This diversity may account for much of the disagreement within stress research. Part of the solution to this problem lies with agreeing the theoretical framework within which measurement is made, but part lies with the development of a more adequate technology of measurement based in 'good practice' in a number of areas including psychometrics, knowledge elicitation and knowledge modelling. A forced standardisation of measurement is *not* being argued for here and should be resisted for its effects on scientific progress. What *is* be-

8.4

STRESS MANAGEMENT INTERVENTIONS

There have been a wide variety of different interventions which have been advanced as 'stress management', and many others which could have been so labelled but which have not been. A basic distinction can be made between those targeted on the organisation and those targeted on individual workers, and, among the latter, interventions concerned with white-collar and managerial workers are more common than those concerned with blue-collar workers. Various explanations, largely focused on economic and political issues, have been advanced to account for this difference (see also section 8.6).

A review of the scientific literature suggests that there are a number of problems with research into the management of work-related stress. First, too narrow a view has often been taken of what constitutes stress management and there has

been too strong a focus on 'caring for or curing' the *individual*. In many situations, this has reduced the whole issue to one of personnel administration, welfare and counselling. Second, much of what has been offered, even in this narrow respect, has either a weak theoretical base or has been developed from theory outside occupational stress research. Third, there has been a tendency to treat the application of stress management strategies as a self-contained action and to divorce that application from any preceding process of problem diagnosis. Fourth, stress management strategies often focus on single types of intervention and multiple strategies are rarely offered. Last, such interventions are rarely offered for evaluation beyond participants' immediate reactions or measures of face validity (see section 8.5).

There are several overarching reasons why the practice of stress management has been so poor: most relate to the lack of impact of contemporary stress theory on practice. Theory informs practice, and without progress in the development of theory there cannot be a strong logical development of practice. The lack of impact, in turn, may be accounted for partly by the stagnation of theory referred to in section 3, and partly by the lack of a framework which allows the translation of theory into practice. As Kurt Lewin put it, "there's nothing so practical as a good theory".

8.5

EVALUATION OF
INTERVENTIONS

Evaluation has been variously defined. Nutt (1981) has talked of it in terms of the measurement of the degree to which objectives have been achieved, and Green (1974) as the comparison of an object of interest against a standard of acceptability. In contrast to basic research, evaluation implies and requires from the onset criteria and procedures for making judgements of merit, value or worth (Scriven, 1967).

There are three common purposes for evaluations of stress management programmes. The first is to ask whether the programme is effective; specifically whether the programme objectives are being met. A second purpose is to determine the efficiency or comparative effectiveness of two or more programmes or methods within a programme. The third purpose is to assess the cost-benefit or the cost-effectiveness of the programme.

Evaluation data on stress management programmes are relatively rare. There are relatively fewer cost-benefit and cost-effectiveness studies compared to studies on the overall effectiveness of programmes or the relative effectiveness of their component parts (see section 7.5). What there is suggests that stress management programmes may be effective in improving the quality of working life of workers and their immediate psychological health, albeit self-reported. The evidence relating such interventions to improvements in physical health is weaker, largely for methodological reasons. There have been several authoritative reviews of organisational and personal stress management programmes in the last ten years reaching broadly similar conclusions. The publication by the International Labour Organization in 1992, titled 'Preventing Stress at Work', reviews a wide range of different interventions, both completed and in progress, and summarises them in terms of Karasek's (1979) model of job demands/job decision latitude.

There is an obvious need to encourage theoretically exciting and methodologically adequate research in this area of practice. The main problems, which again are widely recognised, relate to: the lack of application of theory to practice, the lack of a framework for practice, the lack of adequately designed and meaningful evaluation studies, and the lack of balance between the number of individually- and organisationally-focused interventions.

In summary, it must be concluded that "the jury is still out" on stress management training: whilst it seems logical that such interventions should promote employee health, there are not yet sufficient data to be confident that they do. However, the evidence for employee assistance programmes –particularly those broadly conceived to include health promotion in the workplace– may be more encouraging, although that which relates to counselling alone is weak. The provision of counselling is largely designed to assist employees who are already experiencing problems, and is, in that sense, post hoc. Stressor reduction / hazard control is, for several reasons, the most promising area for interventions, although, again, there is not yet sufficient information to be confident about the nature and extent of their effectiveness. To date, such conclusions are based more on moral and strategic reasoning than on empirical data, although the data that do exist are supportive. What can be firmly concluded, however, is that there is still a need for further and more adequate evaluation studies. Perhaps the key to the methodology and evaluation of intervention studies is a re-appraisal of the value of the natural science paradigm in field research (Griffiths, 1999b). One issue might be the inappropriateness of the evaluation paradigm itself.

8.6

INDIVIDUAL- AND ORGANISATIONAL-LEVEL INTERVENTIONS

Unfortunately, there are very few well de-signed and evaluated interventions available in the literature to date (see section 7). Nonetheless, Murphy et al. (1992) con-clude that "job redesign and organisation-al change remain the preferred approaches to stress management because they focus on reducing or eliminating the sources of the problem in the work environment". However, they also point out that such ap-proaches require a detailed audit of work stressors and a knowledge of the dynamics of organisational change if unwelcome outcomes are to be minimised. Moreover, such interventions can be expensive and more difficult and disruptive to design, im-plement and evaluate –factors which may make them less popular alternatives to sec-ondary and tertiary interventions.

Nonetheless, Landy (1992) has sum-marised a number of possible interven-tions focused on the design of the work environment, and Murphy (1988) notes that given the varieties of work stressors that have been identified, many other types of action relating to organisational and work development should be effective in reducing work stress. Van der Hek & Plomp (1997) also concluded that "there is some evidence that organization-wide ap-proaches show the best results on individ-ual, individual-organizational interface and organizational parameters [outcome measures]; these comprehensive pro-grammes have a strong impact on the en-tire organization, and require the full support of management". The emerging evidence is strong enough for the United States' National Institute for Occupational Safety and Health (NIOSH) to have identi-fied "the organization of work" as one of the national occupational safety and health priority areas (Rosenstock, 1997). As part of their National Occupational Re-search Agenda (NORA), NIOSH intend to focus research on issues such as the impact of work organisation on overall health, the identification of healthy organisation char-acteristics and the development of inter-vention strategies.

What is not clear from the evaluation liter-ature is the exact mechanism by which such interventions, and particularly those focused on the individual, might affect health. Often, where different types of in-dividually focused interventions have been compared, there is no evidence that any one or any combination is better than any other. This indicates that there may be a general, non-specific effect of intervening. The fact of an intervention may be beneficial, rather than its exact content. Interviews with managers responsible for introducing such interventions suggest that they are aware of such effects (see, for example, Cox *et al.*, 1988). It is therefore possible that at least part of the effects of stress management programmes is due to the way they alter workers' perceptions of and attitudes to their organisations, and hence organisational culture. It was argued earlier that poor organisational culture might be associated with an increased experience of stress, while a good organisational culture might weaken or "buffer" the effects of stress on health. A defining factor for organisational culture is the size of the enterprise, and this should be borne in mind when considering intervention and evaluation issues, together with the wider context in terms of the socio-economic environment in the Member States.

8.7

OVERALL CONCLUSIONS

The evidence on the effectiveness of stress management interventions reviewed in this Status Report is promising. The available data, although sparse, suggest that interventions, especially at the organisational level (e.g., Cox *et al.*, 2000; Ganster *et al.*, 1982; Shinn *et al.*, 1984; Dollard & Winefield, 1996; Kompier *et al.*, 1998), are beneficial to both individual and organisational health and should be investigated –and evaluated– further.

The strategic argument for the management of work stress advanced in this Report on the basis of the available scientific evidence and current legal thinking in Europe is that work stress is a current and future health and safety issue, and, as such, should be dealt with in the same logical and systematic way as other health and safety issues. That is, the management of stress at work should be based on the

adaptation and application of a control cycle approach such as that made explicit in contemporary models of risk management (see section 7.1). This is already happening in several countries of the European Union, for example in the United Kingdom (Cox *et al.*, 2000; Griffiths *et al.*, 1996), the Netherlands (Kompier *et al.*, 1998) and Finland (Elo, 1994). In different countries this approach is given different names, and a wide variety of local arguments are deployed to support its use. However, the underlying philosophy is the same, and this approach offers the best way forward.

The final comment concerns the maturity of stress research as an area of applied science. Two things must be apparent to the informed reader of this Report. First, there is a wealth of scientific data on work stress, its causes and effects, and on some of the mechanisms underpinning the relationships among these. More general research is not needed. What is required is an answer to the outstanding methodological questions, and to more specific questions about particular aspects of the overall stress process and its underpinning mechanisms. Second, although this wealth of scientific data exists, it still needs to be translated into practice, and the effectiveness of this practice evaluated. This is another set of needs, and one that will only be settled outside the laboratory and through the development of consensus and eventually common practice.

While stress at work will remain a major challenge to occupational health, our ability to understand and manage that challenge is improving. The future looks bright.

RESEARCH

9.

REFERENCES

Abel, T.M., Metraux, R., & Roll, S. (1987) Psychotherapy and Culture. University of New Mexico Press, Albuquerque.

Ader, R. A. (1981) Psychoneuroimmunology. Academic Press, New York.

Akerstedt, T., & Landstrom, U. (1998) Work place countermeasures of night shift fatigue International Journal Of Industrial Ergonomics, Vol.21, No.3-4, pp.167-178

Ahasan M.R., Mohiuddin G., Vayrynen S., Ironkannas H., & Quddus R. (1999) Work-related problems in metal handling tasks in Bangladesh: obstacles to the development of safety and health measures. Ergonomics, Vol.42, No.2, pp.385-396

Ahlbom, A., Karasek, R.A., & Theorell, T. (1977) Psychosocial occupational demands and risk for cardio-vascular death. Lakartidningen, 77, 4243-4245.

Althouse, R., & Hurrell, J. J. (1977) An Analysis of Job Stress in Coal Mining. Department of Health, Education and Welfare (NIOSH) publication no: 77-217, US Government Printing Office, Washington DC.

Angus, R. G., & Heslegrave, R. J. (1983) The effects of sleep loss and sustained mental work: implications for command and control performance. In: J. Ernsting (ed) Sustained Intensive Air Operations: Physiological and Performance Aspects. NATO-AGARD Cp - 338. Technical Editing & Reproduction Ltd., London.

Anisman, H., Pizzion, A., & Sklar, L.S. (1980) Coping with stress, norepinephrine depletion, and escape performance. Brain Research, 191, 583-588.

Antelman, S.M. & Caggiula, A.R. (1977) Norephinephrine-dopamine interactions and behaviour. Science, 195, 646-653.

Appley, M. H., & Trumbull, R. (1967) Psychological Stress. Appleton-Century-Crofts, New York.

Arnestad, M., & Aanestad, B. (1985) Work environment at a psychiatric ward: stress, health and immunoglobulin levels. Unpublished PhD thesis, University of Bergen, Bergen.

Arroba, T., & James, K. (1990) Reducing the cost of stress: an organizational model. Personnel Review, 19, 21-27.

Arthur H.M., Garfinkel P.E., Irvine J. (1999) Development and testing of a new hostility scale. Canadian Journal Of Cardiology, Vol.15, No.5, pp.539-544

Aspinwall,L.G., Taylor,S.E. (1997) A stitch in time: Self-regulation and proactive coping. Psychological Bulletin, 121, 417-436

Averill, J.R. (1973) Personal control over aversive stimuli and its relationship to stress. Psychological Bulletin, 80, 286-303.

Bacharach, S. B., Bamberger, P.B., & Conley, S. (1991) Work-home conflict among nurses and engineers: mediating the impact of role stress on burnout and satisfaction at work. Journal of Organizational Behaviour, 12, 39-53.

Baddeley, A. D. (1972) Selective attention and performance in dangerous environments. British Journal of Psychology, 63, 537-546.

Bailey, J. M., & Bhagat, R. S. (1987) Meaning and measurement of stressors in the work environment. In: S. V. Kasl & CL Cooper (eds) Stress and Health: Issues in Research Methodology. Wiley & Sons, Chichester.

Baker, D. B. (1985) The study of stress at work. Annual Review of Public Health, 6, 367-381.

Bandura, A. (1977) Self-efficacy: towards a unifying theory of behavioural change. Psychological Review, 84, 191-215.

Barefoot, J. C., Dahlstrom, W. G., & Williams, R. B. (1983) Hostility, CHD incidence, and total mortality: a 25 year follow up study of 255 physicians. Psychomatic Medicine, 45, 83-90.

Barreto S.M., Swerdlow A.J., Smith PG, Higgins CD (1997) Risk of death from motor-vehicle injury in Brazilian steelworkers: A nested case-control study. International Journal Of Epidemiology, Vol.26, No.4, pp.814-821

Barth, P.S. (1990) Workers' compensation for mental stress cases. Behavioural Sciences and the Law, 8, 358.

Baruch, G. K., & Barnett, R. E. (1987) Role quality and psychological well-being. In: F. J. Cobb (ed) Spouse, Parent, Worker: On Gender and Multiple Roles. Yale University Press, New Haven, Conneticut.

Bastiaans, J. (1982) Consequences of modern terrorism. In L. Goldberger & S.Breznitz (eds) Handbook of Stress: Theoretical and Clinical Aspects. Free Press, New York.

Beale, D., Clarke, D., Cox, T., Leather, P. & Lawrence, C. (1999) System memory in violent incidents: Evidence from patterns of reoccurrence. Journal of Occupational Health Psychology, 4(3), 233-244.

Beale, D., Cox, T., Clarke, D., Lawrence, C. & Leather, P. (1998) Temporal architecture of violent incidents. Journal of Occupational Health Psychology, 3, 65-82.

Beattie, R. T., Darlington, T. G., & Cripps, D. M. (1974) The Management Threshold. British Institute of Management Paper, no: OPN 11., BIM, London.

Beckham, E., & Adams, R. (1984) Coping behavior in depression: report on a new scale. Behavioral Research and Therapy, 22, 71-75.

Beehr, T.A. (1995) Psychological Stress in the Workplace. New York: Routledge.

Beehr, T.A. & Newman, J.E. (1978) Job stress, employee health, and organizational effectiveness: a facet analysis, model and literature review. Personnel Psychology, 31, 665-699.

Beehr, T.A., & O'Hara, K. (1987) Methodological designs for the evaluation of occupational stress interventions. In: S. Kasl & C. Cooper (eds) Stress and Health: Issues in Research Methodology. Wiley & Sons, Chichester.

Bergan, T., Vaernes, R. J., Ingebrigsten, P., Tonder, O., Aakvaag, A., & Ursin, H. (1987) Relationships between work environmental problems and health among Norwegian divers in the North Sea. In: A. Marroni & G. Oriani (eds) Diving and Hyperbaric Medicine. Academic Press, New York.

Berridge, J. & Cooper, C.L. (1993) Stress and coping in US organizations: the role of the Employee Assistance Programme. Work & Stress, 7, 89-102.

Bettenhausen, K.L. (1991) 5 years of groups research - what we have learned and what needs to be addressed. Journal Of Management, 17 (2), pp.345-381

Bhagat, R. S., & Chassie, M. B. (1981) Determinants of organizational commitment in working women: some implications for organizational integration. Journal of Occupational Behaviour, 2, 17-30.

Bhalla, S., Jones, B., & Flynn, D. M. (1991) Role stress among Canadian white-collar workers. Work & Stress, 5, 289-299.

Biersner, R.J., Gunderson, E.K., Ryman, D.H., & Rahe, R.H. (1971) Correlations of Physical Fitness, Perceived Health Status, and Dispenssary Visits with Performance in Stressful Training. USN Medical Neuropsychioatric Research Unit. Technical report no: 71-30. US Navy, Washington DC.

Blank, A.S. (1981) The price of constant vigilance: the Vietman era veteran. Frontiers of Psychiatry, 11, Feb.

Blohmke, M., & Reimer, F. (1980) Krankheit und Beruf. Alfred Huthig Verlag, Heidelberg.

Boggild H. & Knutsson A. (1999) Shift work, risk factors and cardiovascular disease. Scandinavian Journal Of Work Environment & Health, Vol.25, No.2, pp.85-99

Borella P., Bargellini A., Rovesti S., Pinelli M., Vivoli R., Solfrini V., & Vivoli G. (1999) Emotional stability, anxiety, and natural killer activity under examination stress Psychoneuroendocrinology, Vol.24, No.6, pp.613-627

Borg, M.G. (1990) Occupational stress in British educational settings: A review. Educational Psychology, 10 (2) 103-126.

Bosma, H., & Marmot, M.G. (1997) Low job control and risk of coronary heart disease in Whitehall II (prospective cohort) study. British Medical Journal, 314, no. 7080

Bowers, K.S. (1973) Situationalism in psychology: an analysis and critique. Psychological Review, 80, 307-335.

Bradley, G. (1989) Computers and the Psychological Work Environment. Taylor and Francis, London.

Brady, J.V. (1958) Ulcers in 'executive' monkeys. Scientific American, 199, 95-100.

Brady, J.V. (1975) Toward a behavioural biology of emotion. In L. Levi (ed) Emotions: Their Parameters and Measurement. Raven, New York.

Brady, J.V. & Harris, A.H. (1977) The experimental production of altered physiological states. In W. Honig & J.E.R. Staddon (eds) Handbook of Operant Behaviour. Prentice-Hall, Engelwood Cliffs, California.

Brener, J. (1978) Visceral perception. In: J. Beatty (ed) Biofeedback and Behaviour: A NATO Symposium. Plenum Press, New York.

Breslow, L., & Buell, P. (1960) Mortality from coronary heart disease and physical activity of work in California. Journal of Chronic Diseases, 22, 87-91.

Briner, R. (1997) Improving stress assessment: Toward an evidence-based approach to organizational stress interventions. Journal of Psychosomatic Research, 43 (1), 61-71

British Psychological Society (1992) Guidelines for the Prevention and Management of Violence at Work. British Psychological Society, Leicester.

Broadbent, D.E. (1971) Decision and Stress. Academic Press, New York.

Broadbent, D.E., & Gath, D. (1981) Ill health on the line: sorting myth from fact. Employment Gazette, 89, no. 3.

Brook, A. (1973) Mental stress at work. Practitioner, 210, 500-506.

Buck, V. (1972) Working Under Pressure. Staples Press, London.

Bundesministerium für Arbeit und Sozialordnung, 1999. Reported occupational diseases in Germany (1960-1997). Bundesministerium für Arbeit und Sozialordnung.

Burke, R.J. (1986) Occupational and life stress and family: conceptual frameworks and research findings. International Review of Applied Psychology, 35, 347-369.

Burke, R.J. (1993) Organizational-level interventions to reduce occupational stressors. Work and Stress, 7(1), 77-87.

Canadian Mental Health Association (1984) Work and Well-being: The Changing Realities of Employment. Toronto, Ontario.

Cannon, W.B. (1929) Bodily Changes in Pain, Hunger, Fear and Rage: An Account of Recent Researches in the Function of Emotional Excitement. Appleton, New York.

Cannon, W.B., (1931) The Wisdom of the Body. Norton, New York.

Caplan, R.D., Cobb, S., French, J. R. P., van Harrison, R., & Pinneau, S. R. (1975) Job Demands and Worker Health. US Department of Health, Education and Welfare Publication no: NIOSH 75-160, US Government Printing Office, Washington DC.

Carayon, P. (1993) A longitudinal test of Karasek's Job Strain model among office workers. Work & Stress, Vol.7, No.4, pp.299-314

Cartwright, S. & Cooper, CL (1996) Public policy and occupational health psychology in Europe. Journal of Occupational Health Psychology, I (4), 349-361.

Chappell, D. & Di Martino, V. (1998) Violence at Work. Geneva: International Labour Office.

Chatterjee, D.S. (1987) Repetition strain injury - a recent review. Journal of the Society of Occupational Medicine, 37, 100-105.

Chatterjee, D.S. (1992) Workplace upper limb disorders : a prospective study with intervention. Occupational Medicine, 42, 129-136.

Chen, P.Y. & Spector, P.E. (1991) Negative affectivity as the underlying cause of correlations between stressors and strains. Journal of Applied Psychology, 76, 398-407.

Cincirpini, P. M., Hook, J. D., Mendes de Leon, C. F., & Pritchard, W. S. (1984) A Review of cardiovascular, Electromyographic, Electrodermal and Respiratory Measures of Psychological Stress. National Institute for Occupational Safety and Health, contract no: 84-257, Cincinnati, Ohio.

Cobb, S., & Kasl, S. V. (1977) Termination: the Consequences of Job Loss. US Department of Health, Education and Welfare, Cincinnati.

Cohen, A. (1969) Effects of noise on psychological state. In: W. D. Ward & J. E. Fricke (eds) Noise as a Public Health Hazard. American Speech and Hearing Association, Washington DC.

Cohen, A. (1974) Industrial noise and medical, absence and accident record data on exposed workers. In: W. D. Ward (ed) Proceedings of the International Congress on Noise as a Public Health Problem. US Environmental Protection Agency, Washington DC.

Cohen, A. (1976) The influence of a company hearing conservative program on extra-auditory problems in workers. Journal of Safety Research, 8, 146-162.

Cohen, S. (1980) After effects of stress on human performance and social behaviour: a review of research and theory. Psychological Bulletin, 88, 82-108.

Cohen, S.G. & Ledford, G.E. (1994) the effectiveness of self-managing teams - a quasi-experiment. Human Relations, 47 (1), pp.13-43

Cohen, S., & Willis, T. A. (1985) Stress, social support and the buffering hypothesis. Psychological Bulletin, 98, 310-357.

Colligan, M.J., Smith, M.J., & Hurrell, J.J. (1977) Occupational incidence rates of mental health disorders. Journal of Human Stress, 3, 34-39.

Confederation of British Industry [CBI] (1999) Absence Bill Of £10 Billion For Business In 1998 - CBI Survey. Confederation of British Industry, London.

Cooper, C.L. (1978) Work stress. In: P. B. Warr (ed) Psychology at Work. Penguin, Harmondsworth.

Cooper, C.L. (1981) Executive Families Under Stress. Prentice Hall, Englewood Cliffs, New Jersey.

Cooper, C.L. & Cartwright, S. (1997) An intervention strategy for workplace stress. Journal of Psychosomatic Research, 43 (1), 7-16

Cooper, C.L., & Davidson, M. (1982) High Pressure: Working Lives of Women Managers. Fontana, London.

Cooper, C.L., & Hingley, P. (1985) The Change Makers. Harper and Row, London.

Cooper, C.L., & Marshall, J. (1976) Occupational sources of stress: a review of the literature relating to coronary heart disease and mental ill health. Journal of Occupational Psychology, 49, 11-28.

Cooper, C.L., & Smith, M. J. (1986) Job Stress and Blue Collar Work. Wiley & Sons, Chichester.

Cooper, C.L. & Williams, S. (1997) Creating healthy work organizations. Chichester: John Wiley & Sons

Cooper, C.L., Liukkonen, P. & Cartwright, S. (1996) Stress prevention in the work-place: assessing the costs and benefits to organisations. Dublin: European Foundation for the Improvement of Living and Working Conditions.

Cooper, C.L., Allison, T., Reynolds, P., & Sadri, G. (1992a) An individual-based counselling approach for combating stress in British Post Office employees. In International Labour Office, Conditions of Work Digest (Vol. 11): Preventing Stress at Work. International Labour Office, Geneva.

Cooper, C.L., Sadri, G., Allison, T., & Reynolds, P. (1992b) Stress counselling in the Post Office. Counselling Psychology Quarterly, 3, 3-11.

Corey, D.M. & Wolf, G.D. (1992) An integrated approach to reducing stress injuries. In J.C. Quick, L.R. Murphy, & J.J. Hurrell (eds) Stress and Well-being at Work.

Council Directive 89/391/EEC of 12 June 1989 on the introduction of measures to encourage improvements in the safety and health of workers at work. Official Journal L 183, 29/06/1989 p. 0001 – 0008 Internet WWW page at http://europa.eu.int/eur-lex/en/lif/dat/1989/en_389L0391.html

Council Directive 98/24/EC of 7 April 1998 on the protection of the health and safety of workers from the risks related to chemical agents at work (fourteenth individual Directive within the meaning of Article 16(1) of Directive 89/391/EEC). Official Journal L 131, 05/05/1998 p. 0011 – 0023 Internet WWW page at http://europa.eu.int/eur-lex/en/lif/dat/1998/en_398L0024.html

Cox, S., & Tait, R. (1991) Safety, Reliability and Risk Management. Butterworth Heinemann, London.

Cox, S., Cox, T., Thirlaway, M., & Mackay, C. J. (1985) Effects of simulated repetitive work of urinary catecholamine excretion. Ergonomics, 25, 1129-1141.

Cox, T. (1978) Stress. Macmillan, London.

Cox, T. (1980) Repetitive work. In: CL Cooper & R. Payne (eds) Current Concerns in Occupational stress. Wiley & Sons, Chichester.

Cox, T. (1984) Stress: a psychophysiological approach to cancer. In: CL Cooper (ed) Psychosocial Stress and Cancer. Wiley & Sons, Chichester.

Cox, T. (1985a) The nature and measurement of stress. Ergonomics, 28, 1155-1163.

Cox, T. (1985b) Repetitive work: occupational stress and health. In: CL Cooper & M. J. Smith (eds) Job Stress and Blue Collar Work. Wiley & Sons, Chichester.

Cox, T. (1987). Stress, coping and problem solving. Work & Stress, 1, 5-14.

Cox, T. (1988a) Psychobiological factors in stress and health. In S. Fisher & J. Reason (eds) Handbook of Life Stress, Cognition and Health. Wiley & Sons, Chichester.

Cox, T. (1988b) AIDS and stress. Work & Stress, 2, 109-112.

Cox, T. (1990) The recognition and measurement of stress: conceptual and methodological issues. In: E. N. Corlett & J. Wilson (eds) Evaluation of Human Work. Taylor & Francis, London.

Cox, T. (1993) Stress Research and Stress Management: Putting theory to work. Sudbury: HSE Books.

Cox, T., & Cox, S. (1985) The role of the adrenals in the psychophysiology of stress. In: E. Karas (ed) Current Issues in Clinical Psychology. Plenum Press, London.

Cox, T. & Cox, S. (1992) Mental health at work: assessment and control. In R. Jenkins & N. Coney (eds) Prevention of Mental Ill Health at Work. HMSO, London.

Cox, T., & Cox, S. (1993) Psychosocial and Organizational Hazards: Monitoring and Control. Occasional Series in Occupational Health, No.5. World Health Organization (Europe), Copenhagen, Denmark.

Cox, T., & Ferguson, E. (1991) Individual differences, stress and coping. In: CL Cooper & R. Payne (eds) Personality and Stress. Wiley & Sons, Chichester.

Cox, T., & Ferguson, E. (1994) Measurement of the subjective work environment. Work & Stress, 8 (2), 98-109

Cox, T. & Griffiths, A.J. (1994) The nature and measurement of work stress: Theory and practice. In N. Corlett & J. Wilson (Eds.) Evaluation of Human Work: A Practical Ergonomics Methodology. London: Taylor and Francis.

Cox, T. & Griffiths, A.J. (1995) The assessment of psychosocial hazards at work. In M.J. Shabracq, J.A.M. Winnubst & CL Cooper (Eds.) Handbook of Work and

Health Psychology. Chichester: Wiley & Sons

Cox, T., & Howarth, I. (1990) Organizational health, culture and helping. Work & Stress, 4, 107-110.

Cox, T., & Kuk, G (1991) Healthiness of schools as organizations: teacher stress and health. Paper to: International Congress, Stress, Anxiety & Emotional Disorders, University of Minho, Braga, Portugal.

Cox, T., & Leather, P. (1994) The prevention of violence at work: application of a cognitive behavioural theory. In: CL Cooper & I. Robertson (eds) International Review of Industrial and Organizational Psychology, Wiley & Sons, Chichester.

Cox, T., & Leiter, M. (1992) The health of healthcare organizations. Work & Stress, 6, 219-227.

Cox, T., & Mackay, C. J. (1981) A transactional approach to occupational stress. In: E. N. Corlett and J. Richardson (eds) Stress, Work Design and Productivity. Wiley & Sons, Chichester.

Cox, T., & Mackay, C. J. (1982) Psychosocial factors and psychophysiological mechanisms in the aetiology and development of cancers. Social Science and Medicine, 16, 381-396.

Cox, T., & Mackay, C.J. (1985) The measurement of self-reported stress and arousal. British Journal of Psychology, 76, 183-186.

Cox, T. & Thomson, L. (2000) Organisational healthiness: work-related stress and employee health. In P. Dewe, M. Leiter & T.

Cox (Eds.) Coping, Health and Organisations. London: Taylor & Francis.

Cox, T., Cox, S., & Thirlaway, M. (1983) The psychological and physiological response to stress. In: A. Gale & J. A. Edwards (eds) Physiological Correlates of Human Behaviour. Academic Press, London.

Cox, T., Ferguson, E., & Farnsworth, W. F. (1993) Nurses' knowledge of HIV and AIDS and their perceptions of the associated risk of infection at work. Paper to: VI European Congress on Work and Organizational Psychology, Alicante.

Cox, T., Leather, P., & Cox, S. (1990) Stress, health and organizations. Occupational Health Review, 23, 13-18.

Cox, T., Watts, C., & Barnett, A. (1981) The Experience and Effects of Task-Inherent Demand. Final technical report to the US Army Research, Development and Standardization Group (UK).

Cox, T., Griffiths, A.J., Barlow, C.A., Randall, R.J., Thomson, L.E. & Rial-Gonzalez, E. (2000) Organisational interventions for work stress: a risk management approach. HSE Books, Sudbury.

Crown, S., Crown, J.M., & Fleming, A. (1975) Aspects of the psychology and epidemiology of rheumatoid disease. Psychological Medicine, 5, 291-299.

Danna, K. & Griffin R.W. (1999) Health and well-being in the workplace: A review and synthesis of the literature. Journal Of Management, Vol.25, No.3, pp.357-384

Davidson, M.J., & Cooper, C.L. (1981) A model of occupational stress. Journal of Occupational Medicine, 23, 564-570.

Davidson, M.J., & Cooper, C.L. (1983) Working women in the European Community – the future prospects. Long Range Planning, 16, 49-54.

Davidson, M. J., & Earnshaw, J. (1991) Vulnerable Workers: Psychosocial and Legal Issues. Wiley & Sons, Chichester.

Davies, N.V. & Teasdale, P (1994) The costs to the British economy of work accidents and work-related ill health. Sudbury: HSE Books.

DeFrank, R.S., & Cooper, C.L. (1987) Worksite management interventions: their effectiveness and conceptualization. Journal of Managerial Psychology, 2, 4-10.

Deloitte & Touche Consulting Group (1999) Call Centre Agent Report: A survey on Profit and Productivity. Deloitte Touche Tohmatsu, Melbourne. Internet WWW page at http://www.deloitte.com.au/content/call_centre_survey98.asp

Dembrowski, T.M., MacDougall, J. M., Williams, R. B., Haney, T. L., & Blumenthal, J. A. (1985) Components of Type A hostility and anger-in: relationship to angiographic findings. Psychomatic Medicine, 47, 219-233.

de Rijk, A. J., le Blanc, P. M., Schaufeli, W. B., & de Jonge, J. (1998) Active coping and need for control as moderators of the job demand-control model: effects on burnout. Journal of Occupational and Organizational Psychology, 71, 1-18.

Devereux J., Buckle P. & Vlachonikolis I.G. (1999) Interactions between physical and psychosocial risk factors at work increase the risk of back disorders: an epidemiological approach. Occupational and Environmental Medicine, vol. 56, no. 5, pp. 343-353

Dewe, P. (1987) New Zealand ministers of religion: identifying sources of stress and coping strategies. Work & Stress, 1, 351-363.

Dewe, P. (1991) Measuring work stressors: the role of frequency, duration and demand. Work & Stress, 5, 77-91.

Dewe, P. (1993) Work, stress and coping: common pathways for future research? Work & Stress, 7 (1), 1-3.

Dewe, P. (2000) Measures of coping with stress at work: a review and critique. In P. Dewe, M. Leiter & T. Cox (Eds.) Coping, Health and Organisations. London: Taylor & Francis.

Dewe, P., Cox, T., & Ferguson, E. (1993) Individual strategies for coping with stress at work: a review of progress and directions for future research. Work & Stress, 7 (1), 5-15.

Dewe, P., Leiter, M & Cox, T (Eds.) (2000) Coping, Health and Organisations. London: Taylor & Francis.

Diament, J., & Byers, S. O. (1975) A precise catecholamine assay for small samples. Journal of Laboratory and Clinical Medicine, 85, 679-693.

Dimsdale, J. E., & Moss, J. (1980a) Plasma catecholamines in stress and exercise.

Journal of the American Medical Association, 243, 340-342.

Dimsdale, J. E., & Moss, J. (1980b) Short-term catecholamine response to psychological stress. Psychosomatic Medicine, 42, 493-497.

Dohrenwend, B. S., & Dohrenwend, B. P. (1974) Stressful Life Events: Their Nature and Effects. Wiley & Sons, New York.

Dohrenwend, B.S., Krasnoff, L., Askenasy, A.R. & Dohrenwend, B.P. (1982) The psychiatric epidemiology research interview life events scale

Dohrenwend, B. S., Krasnoff, L., Askenasy, A. R., & Dohrenwend, B. P. (1988) The Psychiatric Epidemiology Research Interview Life Events Scale. In: L. Goldberg & S. Breznitz (eds) Handbook of Stress: Theoretical and Clinical Aspects. Free Press, New York.

Dollard, M.F. & Winefield, A.H. (1996) Managing occupational stress: a national and international perspective. International Journal of Stress Management, 3 (2), 69-83.

Donaldson, J., & Gowler, D. (1975) Perogatives, participation and managerial stress. In: D. Gowler & K. Legge (eds) Managerial Stress. Gower Press, London.

Douglas, M. (1992) Risk and Blame. Routledge, London.

Eaton, W.W., Anthony, J.C., Mandel, W., & Garrison, R. (1990) Occupation and prevalence of major depressive disorder. Journal of Occupational Medicine, 32, 1079-1086.

Edwards, J.R. & Cooper, C.L. (1990) The person-environment fit approach to stress: recurring problems and some suggested solutions. Journal of Organizational Behaviour, 11, 293-307.

Einhorn, H.J., & Hogarth, R.M. (1981) Behavioural decision theory: processes of judgement and choice. Annual Review of Psychology, 32, 53-88.

Ekehammer, B. (1974) Interactionism in personality from a historical perspective. Psychological Bulletin, 81, 1026.

Elkin, A.J. & Rosch, P.J. (1990) Promoting mental health at the workplace: the prevention side of stress management. Occupational Medicine State of the Art review. 5(4), 739-754

Ellertsen, B., Johnsen, T. B., & Ursin, H. (1978) Relationship between the hormonal responses to activation and coping. In: H. Ursin, E. Baade, and S. Levine (eds) Psychobiology of Stress: A Study of Coping Men. Academic Press, New York.

Elo, A.-L. (1986) Assessment of Psychic Stress Factors at Work. Institute of Occupational Health, Helsinki.

Elo, A.-L. (1994) Assessment of mental stress factors at work. Occupational Medicine, 945-959

Endresen, I.M., Ellertsen, B., Endresen, C., Hjelmen, A.M., Matre, R., & Ursin, H. (1991) Stress at work and psychological and immunological parameters in a group of Norwegian female bank employees. Work & Stress, 5, 217-227.

Endresen, I. M., Vaernes, R. J., Ursin, H., & Tonder, O. (1987) Psychological stress factors and concentration of immunoglobulins and complement components in Norwegian nurses. Work & Stress, 1, 365-375.

Ertel, M., Junghanns, G., Pech, E., & Ullsperger, P. (1997) Auswirkungen der Bildschirmarbeit auf Gesundheit und Wohlbefinden. Wirtschaftsverlag NW, Bremerhaven. (Schriftenreihe der Bundesanstalt für Arbeitsmedizin: Forschung, Fb 762)

European Agency for Safety and Health at Work (1998) Priorities and Strategies in OSH Policy in the Member States of the EU. European Agency for Safety and Health at Work, Bilbao. Internet WWW page at http://agency.osha.eu.int/reports/priorities (available in 8 EU languages)

European Agency for Safety and Health at Work (1999) Work-related neck and upper limb musculoskeletal disorders. Luxembourg: Office for Official Publications of the European Communities.

European Commission (1996) Guidance on risk assessment at work. European Commission, Brussels.

European Foundation for the Improvement of Living and Working Conditions (1992) European Survey on the Work Environment . Dublin, Ireland.

European Foundation for the Improvement of Living and Working Conditions (1996) Second European Survey on Working Conditions in the European Union. Dublin, Ireland

European Foundation for the Improvement of Living and Working Conditions (1997) European Working Environment in Figures. Dublin, Ireland

Eysenck, M. W. (1983) Anxiety and individual differences. In: G. R. J. Hockey (ed) Stress and Fatigue in Human Performance. Wiley & Sons, Chichester.

Feather, N.T. (1990) The Psychological Impact of Unemployment. Springer-Verlag, New York.

Feldman, S. (1991) Today's EAP's make the grade. Personnel, 68, 3-40.

Ferguson, D. (1973) A study of occupational stress and health. Ergonomics, 16, 649-663.

Ferguson, E., & Cox, T. (1993) Exploratory factor analysis: a user's guide. International Journal of Selection and Assessment, 1 (2), 84-94

Fielden S.L & Peckar C.J. (1999) Work stress and hospital doctors: a comparative study. Stress Medicine, vol. 15, no. 3, pp. 137-141

Figley, C.R. (1985) Trauma and Its Wake: The Study of Treatment of Post Traumatic Stress Disorder. Brunner/Mazel, New York.

Fisher, S. (1986). Stress and Strategy. Lawrence Erlbaum Associates, London.

Fisher, S. (1996) Life change, personal control and disease. South African Journal of Psychology, Vol.26, No.1, pp.16-22

Flanagan, P., McAnally, K.I., Martin, R.L., Meehan, J.W., & Oldfield S.R. (1998) Aurally and visually guided visual search in a virtual environment. Human Factors, Vol.40, No.3, pp.461-468.

Fletcher, B. C. (1988) The epidemiology of occupational stress. In: C.L. Cooper & R. Payne (eds) Causes, Coping and Consequences of Stress at Work. Wiley & Sons, Chichester.

Folger, R., & Belew, J. (1985) Nonreactive measurement: a focus for research on absenteeism and occupational stress. In: L. L. Cummings & B. M. Straw (eds) Organizational Behaviour. JAI Press Inc., Greenwich, Connecticut.

Folkard, S., & Monk, T. H. (1985) Hours of Work - Temporal Factors in Work Scheduling. Wiley & Sons, Chichester.

Folkman, S. (1984). Personal control and stress and coping processes: a theoretical analysis. Journal of Personality and Social Psychology, 46, 839-852.

Folkman, S., & Lazarus, R. (1986). Stress process and depressive symptomology. Journal of Abnormal Psychology, 95 , 107-113.

Folkman, S., Lazarus, R., Greun, R., & DeLongis, A. (1986b). Appraisal, coping, health status, and psychological symptoms. Journal of Personality and Social Psychology, 50, 571-579.

Folkman, S., Lazarus, R.S., Dunkel-Schetter, C,. DeLongis, A., & Gruen, R. (1986a). Dynamics of a stressful encounter: cognitive appraisal, coping, and encounter outcomes. Journal of Personality and Social Psychology. 50, 992-1003.

Forsythe, R.P., & Harris, R.E. (1970) Circulatory changes during stressful stimuli in rhesus monkeys. Circulation Research (supp. 1) 26-27, I.B-I.20.

Fox, B. H. (1981) Psychosocial factors and the immune system in human cancer. In: R. Ader (ed) Psychoneuroimmunology. Academic Press, New York.

Frankenhauser, M. (1975) Sympathetic-adreno-medullary activity, behaviour and the psychosocial environment. In: P. H. Venables & M. Christie (eds) Research in Psychophysiology. Wiley & Sons, Chichester.

Frankenhauser, M., & Gardell, B. (1975) Underload and overload in working life: a multidisciplinary approach. Reports from the Department of Psychology, no: 460, University of Stockholm, Stockholm.

Frankenhauser, M., & Gardell, B. (1976) Underload and overload in working life: outline of a multidisciplinary approach. Journal of Human Stress, 2, 15-23.

French, J. R. P., & Caplan, R. D. (1970) Psychosocial factors in coronary heart disease. Industrial Medicine, 39, 383-397.

French, J. R. P., & Caplan, R. D. (1972) Organizational stress and individual strain. In: A. Marrow (ed) The Failure of Success. AMACOM, New York.

French, J. R. P., Caplan, R. D., & van Harrison, R. (1982) The Mechanisms of Job Stress and Strain. Wiley & Sons, New York.

French, J. R. P., Rogers, W., & Cobb, S. (1974) A model of person-environment fir. In: G.W. Coehlo, D.A. Hamburg, & J.E. Adams, (eds) Coping and Adaptation. Basic Books, New York.

Frese, M. & Zapf, D. (1988) Methodological issues in the study of work stress: Objective vs. subjective measurement of work stress and the question of longitudinal studies. In CL Cooper & R. Payne (Eds.) Causes, Coping and Consequences of Stress at Work. Chichester: John Wiley.

Friedman, M., & Rosenman, R.H. (1974) Type A: Your Behaviour and Your Heart. Knoft, New York.

Friedman, M., & Ulmer, D. (1984) Treating Type A Behaviour and Your Behaviour. Knoft, New York.

Gael, S. (1988) The Job Analysis Handbook for Business, Industry and Government. Wiley & Son, New York.

Ganster, D.C., & Fusilier, M.R. (1989) Control in the workplace. In: CL Cooper & I. Robertson (eds) International Review of Industrial and Organizational Psychology. Wiley & Sons, Chichester.

Ganster, D.C., Mayes, B.T., & Fuselier, M.R. (1986) Role of social support in the experience of stress at work. Journal of Applied Psychology, 71, 102-110.

Ganster, D.C., Mayes B.T., Sime W.E., & Tharp GD (1982) Managing occupational stress: a field experiment. Journal of Applied Psychology, 67, 533-542.

Gardell, B. (1971) Alienation and mental health in the modern industrial environ-

ment. In: L. Levi (ed) Society, Stress and Disease Vol I. Oxford University Press, Oxford.

Gardell, B. (1973) Quality of Work and Non-work Activities and Rewards in Affluent Societies. Reports from Psychological Laboratories no: 403, University of Stockholm, Stockholm.

Gardell, B. (1982) Work participation and autonomy: A multilevel approach to democracy at the workplace. International Journal of Health Services, 12, 31-41.

Gardiner, B.M. (1980) Psychological aspects of rheumatoid arthritis. Psychological Medicine, 10, 150-163.

Genest, M. (1983) Coping with rheumatoid arthritis. Canadian Journal of Behavioural Science, 15, 392-408.

Genest, M. (1989) The relevance of stress to rheumatoid arthritis. In R.W.J. Neufeld (ed) Advances in the Investigation of Psychological Stress.Wiley & sons, New York.

Geurts S., Rutte C., & Peeters M. (1999) Antecedents and consequences of work-home interference among medical residents. Social Science & Medicine, Vol.48, No.9, pp.1135-1148

Glass, D. C. (1977) Behaviour Patterns, Stress and Coronary Disease. Erlbaum, Hillsadle, New Jersey.

Glass, D. C., & Singer, J. E. (1972) Urban Stress: Experiments on Noise and Social Stressors. Academic Press, New York.

Gobel M, Springer J, Scherff J (1998) Stress and strain of short haul bus drivers: Psychophysiology as a design oriented method for analysis. Ergonomics, Vol.41, No.5, pp.563-580

Goldberg, R.J. & Novack, D.H. (1992) The psychosocial review of systems. Social Science & Medicine, Vol.35, No.3, pp.261-269

Goldenhar, L. M., Swanson, N. G. Hurrell Jnr., J. J., Ruder, A. & Deddens, J. (1998). Stressors and adverse outcomes for female construction workers. Journal of Occupational Health Psychology, 3, 19 - 32.

Golembiewski, R.T., Hilles, R, & Daly, R (1987) Some effects of multiple OD interventions on burnout and work site features. Journal of Applied Behavioral Science, 23, 295-313

Green, L. W. (1974) Towards cost-benefit evaluations of health education. Health Education Monographs, 1 (Supplement), 34-36.

Griffiths, A.J. (1999a) Work design and management - The older worker. Experimental Aging Research, 25 (4), pp.411-420

Griffiths, A.J. (1999b) Organizational interventions: facing the limits of the natural science paradigm. Scandinavian Journal of Work and Environmental Health, 25(6), pp. 589-596.

Griffiths, A.J., Cox, T. & Auty A. (1998) Work stress: a brief guide for line managers. Loss Prevention Council, Borehamwood, UK.

Griffiths, A.J., Cox, T. & Barlow, C.A. (1996) Employers' responsibilities for the assessment and control of work-related stress: a European perspective. Health and Hygiene, 17, 62-70.

Guppy, A., Weatherstone, L. (1997) Coping strategies, dysfunctional attitudes and psychological well-being in white collar public sector employees. Work And Stress, 11,58-67

Gutek, B. A., Repetti, R. L., & Silver, D. L. (1988) Nonwork roles and stress at work. In: CL Cooper & R. Payne (eds) Causes, coping and Consequences of Stress at Work. Wiley & Sons, Chichester.

Hacker, W. (1991) Objective work environment: analysis and evaluation of objective work characteristics. Paper presented to: A Healthier Work Environment: Basic Concepts & Methods of Measurement. Hogberga, Lidingo, Stockholm.

Hacker, W., Iwanova, A., & Richter, P. (1983) Tatigkeits-bewertungssystem (TBS-L). Hogrefe, Gottingen.

Hall, E.M. (1991) Gender, work control and stress: a theoretical discussion and an empirical test. In J.V. Johnson & G. Johansson (eds) The Psychosocial Work Environment: Work Organization, Democratization and Health. Baywood Publishing, New York.

Handy, C. (1975) Difficulties of combining family and career. The Times, Sept 22, 16.

Harrington, J. M. (1978) Shift Work and Health: A critical review of the Literature. HMSO, London.

Harris, L. & Associates (1985) Poll conducted for the Metropolitan Life Foundation

Hart, K.E. (1987) Managing stress in occupational settings: a selective review of current research and theory. In CL Cooper (ed) Stress Management Interventions at Work. MCB University Press Ltd.

Haslam, D. R. (1982) Sleep loss, recovery sleep and military performance. Ergonomics, 25, 163-178.

Haynes, S.G., Feinleib, M. , Levine, S., Scotch, N., & Kannel, W.B. (1978b) The relationship of psychosocial factors to coronary heart disease in the Framingham study, II. Prevalence of coronary heart disease. American Journal of Epidemiology, 107, 384-402.

Haynes, S.G., Levine, S., Scotch, N., Feinleib, M., & Kannel, W.B. (1978a) The relationship of psychosocial factors to coronary heart disease in the Framingham study, I. American Journal of Epidemiology, 107, 362-383.

Health & Safety Executive (1990a) Work Related Upper Limb Disorders : A Guide to Prevention. HSE Books, Sudbury.

Health & Safety Executive (1990b) Mental Health at Work.HSE Books, Sudbury.

Heinisch, D.A. & Jex, S.M. (1998) Measurement of negative affectivity: a comparison of self-reports and observer ratings. Work & Stress, 12 (2), 145-160.

Henry, J. P., & Stephens, P. M. (1977) Stress, Health and the Social Environment. A Sociobiologic Approach to Medicine. Springer, New York.

Hiebert, B. & Farber, I. (1984) Teacher stress: A literature survey with a few surprises. Canadian Journal of Education, 9 (1), 14-27.

Hillas, S., & Cox, T. (1987) Post Traumatic Stress Disorder in the Police. Occasional Paper. Police Scientific Research and Development Branch, Home Office, London.

Hingley, P., & Cooper, C.L. (1986) Stress and the Nurse Manager. Wiley & Son, Chichester.

Holmes, T. H., & Rahe, R. H. (1967) The Social Readjustment Rating Scale. Journal of Psychosomatic Research, 11, 213-218.

Holroyd, K.A., & Lazarus, R.S. (1982) Stress, coping and somatic adaptation. In: L. Goldberger & S. Breznitz (eds) Handbook of Stress: Theoretical and Clinical Aspects. Free Press, New York.

Holt, R. R. (1982) Occupational stress. In: L. Goldberger & S. Breznitz (eds) Handbook of Stress: Theortical and Clinical Aspects. Free Press, New York.

House, J. (1974) Occupational stress and coronary heart disease: a review and theoretical integration. Journal of Health and Social Behaviour, 15, 12-27.

House, J. S., & Wells, J. A. (1978) Occupational stress, social support and health. In: A. McLean, G. Black, & M. Colligan (eds) Reducing Occupational Stress: Proceedings of a Conference. DWEH (NIOSH) Publication no: 78-140, 8-29.

House, J.S., McMichael, A.J., Wells, J.A., Kaplan, B.H., & Landerman, L.R. (1979) Occupational stress and health among factory workers. Journal of Health and Social Behaviour,20, 139-160.

Houts, P. S., & McDougall, V.C. (1988) Effects of informing workers of their health risks from exposure to toxic materials. American Journal of Industrial Medicine, 13, 271-279.

Hurrell, J. J., & McLaney, M. A. (1989) Control, job demands and job satisfaction. In: S. L. Sauter, J. J. Hurrell, & CL Cooper (eds) Job Control and Worker Health. Wiley & Sons, Chichester.

Idzikowski, C., & Baddeley, A. D. (1983) Fear and dangerous environments. In: G. R. J. Hockey (ed) Stress and Fatigue in Human Performance. Wiley & Sons, Chichester.

Ilmarinen J., & Rantanen J. (1999) Promotion of work ability during ageing. American Journal of Industrial Medicine, No.S1, pp.21-23

Ingersoll G.L., Cook J.A., Fogel S., Applegate M, Frank B (1999) The effect of patient-focused redesign on midlevel nurse managers' role responsibilities and work environment. Journal Of Nursing Administration, Vol.29, No.5, pp.21-27

International Federation of Commercial, Clerical and Technical Employees [FIET] (1992) Resolutions adopted by the 22nd FIET World Congress (San Fransisco, August 1991). Geneva.

International Labour Organization [ILO] (1986) Psychosocial Factors at Work: Recognition and Control. Occupational Safety and Health Series no: 56, International Labour Office, Geneva.

International Labour Organization [ILO] (1992) Preventing Stress at Work. Conditions of Work Digest, 11, International Labour Office, Geneva.

Intindola, B. (1991) EAP's still foreign to many small businesses. National Underwriter, 95, 21.

Irwin, J., & Anisman, H. (1984) Stress and pathology: immunological and central nervous system interactions. In: CL Cooper (ed) Psychosocial Stress and Cancer. Wiley & Sons, Chichester.

Israel, B.A., Baker, E.A., Goldenhar, L.M., Heaney, C.A. & Schurman, S.J. (1996) Occupational stress, safety and health: Conceptual framework and principles for effective prevention interventions. Journal of Occupational Health Psychology, I (3), 261-286.

Ivancevich, J.M., & Matteson, M.T. (1980) Stress and Work. Scott Foresman, Glenview, Illinois.

Ivancevich, J.M., & Matteson, M.T. (1986) Organizational level stress management interventions: review and recommendations. Journal of Organizational Behaviour and Management, 8, 229-248.

Ivancevich, J.M., Matteson, M.T., Freedman, S.M., & Phillips, J.S. (1990) Worksite stress management interventions. American Psychologist, 45, 252-261.

Jackson, P. R., & Warr, P. B. (1984) Unemployment and psychological ill health: the moderating role of duration and age. Psychological Medicine, 14, 610-614.

Jackson, S. (1983) Participation in decision-making as a strategy for reducing job-related strain. Journal of Applied Psychology, 68, 3-19.

Jackson, S., & Schuler, R. S. (1985) A meta-analysis and conceptual critique of research on role ambiguity and role conflict in work settings. Organizational Behaviour and Human Decision Processes, 36, 16-78.

Jenkins, C.D., Rosenman, R. H., & Friedman, M. (1968) Replicability of rating the coronary prone behaviour pattern. Journal of Chronic Diseases, 20, 371-379.

Jenkins, C.D., Zyzanski, S.J., & Rosenman, R.H. (1976) Risk of new myocardial infarction in middle-aged men with manifest coronary heart disease. Circulation, 53, 342-347.

Jenkins, R. (1992) Prevalence of Mental Illness in the Workplace. In R. Jenkins & N. Coney (eds) Prevention of Mental Ill Health at Work. HMSO, London.

Jex, S.M. (1991) The psychological benefits of exercise in work settings: a review, critique, and dispositional model. Work & Stress, 5, 133-147.

Jex, S.M. & Spector, P.E. (1996) The impact of negative affectivity on stressor-strain relations: a replication and extension. Work & Stress, 10 (1), 36-45.

Jick, T.D. (1979) Mixing qualitative and quantitative methods: Triangulation in action. Administrative Science Quarterly, 24, 602-611.

Johansson, G. & Aronsson, G. (1984) Stress reactions in computerized administrative work. Journal of Occupational Behaviour, 5, 159-181.

Johnson, J. V. (1989) Control, collectivity and the psychosocial work environment. In: S. L. Sauter, J. J. Hurrell Jr & C. L. Cooper (eds) Job control and worker health. John Wiley & Sons, Chichester.

Johnson, J.V. (1996) Conceptual and methodological developments in occupational stress research. An introduction to state-of-the-art reviews I. Journal of Occupational Health Psychology, I (1), 6-8.

Johnson, J.V. & Hall, E.M. (1996) Dialectic between conceptual and causal enquiry in psychosocial work-environment research. Journal of Occupational Health Psychology, I (4), 362-374.

Johnson, J. V., Hall, E. M., Stewart, W., Fredlund, P. & Theorell, T. (1991) Combined exposure do adverse work organization factors and cardiovascular disease: towards a life-course perspective. In: L. D. Fechter (ed.) Proceedings of the 4th International Conference on the Combined Effects of Environmental Factors. Johns Hopkins University Press, Baltimore.

Johnson, L.C. (1981) Biological Rhythms, Sleep and Shift Work. Advances in Sleep Research, Vol 7. Spectrum, New York.

Jones, D.M. (1983) Noise. In: G. R. J. Hockey (ed) Stress and Fatigue in Human Performance. Wiley & Sons, Chichester.

Jones, D.M. (1999) The cognitive psychology of auditory distraction: The 1997 BPS Broadbent Lecture British Journal Of Psychology, 90 (2), 167-187.

Jones, J.R., Hodgson, J.T., Clegg, T.A. & Elliot R.C. (1998) Self-reported work-related illness in 1995: results from a household survey. Sudbury: HSE Books.

Jones, J.W., Barge, B.N., Steffy, B.D., Fay, L.M., Kunz, LK, & Wuebker, LJ (1988) Stress and medical malpractice: organizational risk assessment and intervention. Journal of Applied Psychology, 73, 727-735.

Junghanns, G., Ertel, M., & Ullsperger, P. (1998) Anforderungsbewältigung und Gesundheit bei computergestützter Büroarbeit. Wirtschaftsverlag NW, Bremerhaven. (Schriftenreihe der Bundesanstalt für Arbeitsschutz und Arbeitsmedizin: Forschung, Fb 787)

Junghanns, G.; Ullsperger, P. & Ertel, M. (1999) Zum Auftreten von Gesundheitsbeschwerden bei computergestützter Büroarbeit - eine multivariate Analyse auf der Grundlage einer fragebogengestützten Erhebung. Zeitschrift für Arbeitswissenschaft 53 (25. NF), 18-24.

Junghanns, G., Ullsperger, P., Ertel, M., & Pech, E. (1999, in press) Gesundheit und Wohlbefinden bei moderner Büroarbeit - eine Studie zum "Anforderungs-Kontroll"-Modell. Ergo-Med.

Kahn, R. L. (1973) Conflict, ambiguity and overload: three elements in job stress. Occupational Mental Health, 31, 2-9.

Kahn, R. L. (1974) Conflict, ambiguity and over work: three elements in job stress. In: A. McLean (ed) Occupational Stress. Charles C. Thomas, Springfield, Illinois.

Kahn, R. L., & Byosiere, S. (1990) Stress in Organizations. In: M. Dunnette (ed) Handbook of Industrial and Organizational Psychology. Rand McNally, Chicago.

Kahn, R. L., Wolfe, D. M., Quinn, R. P., Snoek, J. D., & Rosenthal, R. A. (1964) Organizational Stress: Studies in Role Conflict and Ambiguity. Wiley & Sons, New York.

Kang B., Lee B., Kang K.W., Suh J.C., & Yoon ES TI (1999) AHA: a knowledge based system for automatic hazard identification in chemical plant by multimodel approach. Expert Systems With Applications, Vol.16, No.2, pp.183-195

Kanter, R.M. (1977) Work and family in the United States: a critical review and agenda for research and policy. Russell SageFoundation, New York.

Karasek, R. A. (1979) Job demands, job decision latitude and mental strain: implications for job redesign. Administrative Science Quarterly, 24, 285-308.

Karasek, R. A. (1981) Job socialisation and job strain: the implications of two psychosocial mechanisms for job design. In: B. Gardell & G. Johansson (eds) Working Life: A Social Science Contribution to Work Reform. Wiley & Sons, Chichester.

Karasek, R., & Theorell, T. (1990) Healthy Work: Stress, Productivity and the Reconstruction of Working Life. Basic Books, New York.

Karasek, R.A., Schwartz, J., & Theorell, T. (1982) Job characteristics, occupation, and coronary heart disease. (Final report on Grant No. R-01-OH00906). Cincinnati,

OH: National Institute for Occupational Safety and Health.

Karasek, R.A., Baker, D., Marxer, F., Ahlbom, A., & Theorell, T. (1981) Job decision latitude, job demands and cardiovascular disease. American Journal of Public Health, 71, 694-705.

Kasl, S. V. (1980a) Epidemiological contributions to the study of work stress. In: C.L. Cooper and R. Payne (eds) Stress at Work. Wiley & Sons, Chichester.

Kasl, S. V. (1980b) The impact of retirement. In: C.L. Cooper & R.L. Payne (eds) Current Concerns in Occupational Stress. Wiley & Sons, Chichester.

Kasl, S. V. (1984) Stress and health. Annual Review of Public Health, 5, 319-341.

Kasl, S. V. (1987) Methodologies in stress and health: past difficulties, present dilemmas and future directions. In: S. Kasl & C. Cooper (eds) Stress and Health: Issues in Research Methodology. Wiley & Sons, Chichester.

Kasl, S.V. (1989) An epidemiological perspective on the role of control in health. In S.L. Sauter, J.J. Hurrell, & CL Cooper (eds) Job Control and Worker Health. Wiley & Sons, New York.

Kasl, S.V. (1990) Assessing health risks in the work setting. In S. Hobfoll (Ed.) New Directions in Health Psychology Assessment. Washington D.C.: H hemisphere Publishing Corporation.

Kasl, S. V. (1992) Surveillance of psychological disorders in the workplace. In: G. P. Keita & S. L. Sauter (eds) Work and Well-

Being: An Agenda for the 1990s. American Psychological Association, Washington DC.

Kasl, S. V., & Cobb, S. (1967) Effects of parental status incongruence and discrepancy in physical and mental health of adult offspring. Journal of Personality and Social Psychology, monograph: 7, 1-5.

Kasl, S. V., & Cobb, S. (1980) The experience of losing a job: some effects on cardiovascular functioning. Psychotherapy and Psychosomatics, 34, 88-109.

Kasl, S.V. and Cobb, S. (1982) Variability of stress effects among men experiencing job loss. In L. Goldberger & S. Breznitz (eds) Handbook of Stress: Theoretical and Clinical Aspects. Free Press, New York.

Kawakami N, & Haratani T. (1999) Epidemiology of job stress and health in Japan: Review of current evidence and future direction. Industrial Health, Vol.37, No.2, pp.174-186

Kearns, J. (1986) Stress at work: the challenge of change. BUPA series The Management of Health: 1 Stress and the City, BUPA.

Kegeles, S.M., Coates, T., Christopher, A., & Lazarus, J. (1989) Perceptions of Aids: the continuing saga of Aids-related stigma. Aids, 3 (supp 1), S253-S258.

Keita, G. P., & Sauter, S. L. (1992) Work and Well-Being: An Agenda for the 1990s. American Psychological Society, Washington DC.

Kittel, F., Kornitzer, M., DeBacker, B., Dramaix, M., Sobolski, J., Degre, J., Denolin,

H. (1983) Type A in relation to job stress, social and bioclinical variables: the Belgian physical fitness study. Journal of Human Stress, 9, 37-45.

Kobasa, S. (1979). Stressful life events, personality and health: an inquiry into hardiness. Journal of Personality and Social Psychology, 37, 1-13.

Kobasa, S., & Puccetti, M. (1983). Personality and social resources in stress resistance. Journal of Personality and Social Psychology, 45, 839-850.

Kobasa, S., Maddi, S., & Courington, S. (1981). Personality and constitution as mediators in the stress-illness relationship. Journal of Health and Social Behaviour, 22, 368-378.

Kobasa, S., Maddi, S., & Kahn, S., (1982). Hardiness and health: a prospective study. Journal of Personality and Social Psychology, 42, 168-177.

Kobayashi F., Furui H., Akamatsu Y., Watanabe T., & Horibe H. (1999) Changes in psychophysiological functions during night shift in nurses - Influence of changing from a full-day to a half-day work shift before night duty. International Archives of Occupational and Environmental Health, Vol.69, No.2, pp.83-90

Kompier, M.A.J., Geurts, S.A.E., Grundeman, R.W.M., Vink, P. & Smulders, P.G.W. (1998) Cases in stress prevention: the success of a participative and stepwise approach. Stress Medicine, 14, 155-168

Kornhauser, A. (1965) Mental Health of the Industrial Worker. University of Chicago Press, Chicago, Illinois.

Kristensen, T.S. (1996) Job stress and cardiovascular disease: A theoretic critical review. Journal of Occupational Health Psychology, I (3), 246-260.

Kroes, W.H. (1976) Society's victim, the policeman: an analysis of job stress in policing. Thomas, Springfield.

Kryter, K. D. (1972) Non auditory effects of environmental noise. American Journal of Public Health, 62, 389-398.

Kuorinka, I. (1979) Occupational strain from working movments. Paper to: International Ergonomics Association, Warsaw (August). Abstract in: Ergonomics, 22, 732.

Lacey, J. I. (1967) Somatic response patterning and stress: some revisions of activation theory. In: M. H. Appley & R. Trumbull (eds) Psychological Stress. Appleton-Century-Crofts, New York.

Landsbergis, P.A. (1988) Occupational stress among health care workers: a test of the job demands-control model. Journal of Organizational Behaviour, 9, 217-239.

Landsbergis, P.A. & Vivona-Vaughan, E. (1997) Evaluation of an occupational stress intervention in a public agency. Journal of Organizational Behavior, 16, 29-48.

Landsbergis, P.A., Schnall, P.L., Schwartz, J.E., Warren, K. & Pickering, T.G. (1995) Job strain, hypertentsion, and cardiovascular disease: empirical evidence, methodological issues, and recommendations for further research. In S.L. Sauter & L.R. Mur-phy (Eds.) Organizational risk factors for job stress. Washington, DC: APA.

Landstrom, U., Holmberg, K., Kjellberg, A., Soderberg, L., Tesarz, M. (1995) Exposure time and its influence on noise annoyance at work. Journal Of Low Frequency Noise & Vibration, Vol.14, No.4, pp.173-180

Landy, F. J. (1989) The Psychology of Work Behaviour. Brooks/Cole, Monterey, California.

Landy, F. J. (1992) Work design and stress. In: G. P. Keita & S. L. Sauter (eds) Work and Well-Being: An Agenda for the 1990s. American Psychological Association, Washington DC.

Landy, F.J., Quick, J.C. & Kasl, S. (1994) Work, stress and well-being. International Journal of stress management. I (1), 33-73

Larwood, L., & Wood, M. M. (1979) Women in Management. Lexington Books, London.

Last, J. M. (1988) Dictionary of Epidemiol-ogy. Oxford University Press, New York.

Laville, A., & Teiger, C. (1976) Sante men-tale et conditions de travail. Therapeutis-che Umschau, 32, 152-156.

Lazarus, R. S. (1966) Psychological Stress and the Coping Process. McGraw-Hill, New York.

Lazarus, R. S. (1976) Patterns of Adjust-ment. McGraw-Hill, New York.

Lazarus, R.S. & Folkman, S. (1984). Stress, Appraisal and Coping. Springer Publica-tions, New York .

Leather, P., Lawrence, C., Beale, D., Cox, T. & Dickson, R. (1998) Exposure to occupa-tional violence and the buffering effects of intra-organizational support. Work & Stress, 12(2), 161-178.

Leather, P., Brady, C., Lawrence, C., Beale, D. & Cox, T. (Eds.) (1999) Work-related vi-olence: Assessment and intervention. Lon-don: Routledge. ISBN 0415194156.

Leiter, M. (1991) The dream denied: pro-fessional burnout and the constraints of human service organizations. Canadian Psychology, 32, 547-558.

Lennon, M.C. (1999) Work and unemploy-ment as stressors. In Horwitz, Allan V. (Ed); Scheid, Teresa L. (Ed) A handbook for the study of mental health: Social contexts, theories, and systems. (pp. 284-294). New York, NY, USA: Cambridge University Press.

Leventhal, H., and Tomarken, A. (1987) Stress and illness: perspectives from health psychology. In: S. Kasl and C. Cooper (eds) Stress and Health: Issues in Research Methodology. Wiley & Sons, Chichester.

Levi, L. (1972) Stress and distress in re-sponse to psychosocial stimuli. Acta Med-ica Scandinavica, 191, supplement: 528.

Levi, L. (1981) Preventing Work Stress. Ad-dision-Wesley, Reading, Mass.

Levi, L. (1984) Stress in Industry: Causes, Effects and Prevention. Occupational Safety and Health Series no. 51, International Labour Office, Geneva.

Levi, L. (1992) Psychosocial, occupational, environmental and health concepts, research results and applications. In: G.P. Keita and S.L. Sauter (eds) Work and Well Being: An Agenda for the 1990s. American Psychological Association, Washington DC.

Levi, L., Frankenhauser, M., and Gardell, B. (1986) The characteristics of the workplace and the nature of its social demands. In: S. Wolf and A. J. Finestone (eds) Occupational Stress, Health and Performance at Work. PSG Pub. Co. Inc., Littleton, MA.

Lindquist T.L. & Cooper C.L. (1999) Using lifestyle and coping to reduce job stress and improve health in 'at risk' office workers. Stress Medicine, Vol.15, No.3, pp.143-152

Lippe, K. (1990) Compensation for mental-mental claims under Canadian law. Behavioural Sciences and the Law, 8, 398-399.

Lipton, M.A. (1976) Behavioral effects of hypothalamic polypeptide hormones in animals and man. In E.J. Sachar (ed) Hormones, Behaviour and Psychopathology. Raven, New York.

Lisander, B. (1979) Somato-autonomic reactions and their higher control. In C. Brooks, K. Koizumi, and A. Sato (eds) Integrative Functions of the Autonomic Nervous System. Elsevier, New York.

Lobban R.K., Husted J, & Farewell V.T. (1998) A comparison of the effect of job demand, decision latitude, role and supervisory style on self-reported job satisfaction. Work and Stress, Vol.12, No.4, pp.337-350

Locke, A. A. (1976) The nature and causes of job satisfaction. In: M. D. Dunnette (ed) Handbook of Industrial and Organizational Psychology. Rand McNally, Chicago.

Logue, J.N. (1980) Mental health aspects of disaster. Paper presented to the fifth Annual National Hazards Research Workshop, Boulder.

Logue, J.N., Melick, M.E., and Struening, E. (1981) A study of health and mental health status following a major natural disaster. In R. Simmons (ed) Research in Community and Mental Health: An Annual Compilation of Research, Vol. 2. Greewich:, JAI.

Loher, B. T., Noe, R. A., Moeller, N. L., and Fitzgerald, M. P. (1985) A meta-analysis of the relation of job characteristics to job satisfaction. Journal of Applied Psychology, 70, 280-289.

Lu L., Tseng H.J. & Cooper C.L. (1999) Managerial stress, job satisfaction and health in Taiwan Stress Medicine, 1999, Vol.15, No.1, pp.53-64

Lundahl, A. (1971) Fritid Och Rekreation. All Manna Forlager. Laginkomstutredningen, Stockholm.

Lundberg, U., and Forsman, L. (1979) Adrenal medullary and adrenal cortical responses to understimulation and over stimulation: comparison between type A and type B persons. Biological Psychology, 9, 79-89.

MacDougall, J. M., Dembrowski, T. M., Dimsdale, J. E., and Hackett, T. P. (1985) Components of Type A, hostility and anger-in: further relationships to angiographic findings. Health Psychology, 4, 137-152.

Mackay, C. (1987) Violence to Staff in the Health Services. HMSO, London.

Mackay, C., Cox, T., Burrows, G., and Lazzerini, T. (1978) An inventory for the measurement of self-reported stress and arousal. British Journal of Social and Clinical Psychology, 17, 283-284.

MacLennan, B. W. (1992) Stressor reduction: an organizational alternative to individual stress management. In J.C. Quick, L.R. Murphy, JJ. Hurrell (eds) Stress and Well-being at Work: Assessments and Interventions for Occupational Mental Health. American Psychological Association, Washington DC.

Mandler, G. (1982) Stress and thought processes. In: L. Goldberg and S. Breznitz (eds) Handbook of Stress: Theoretical and Clinical Aspects. Free Press, New York.

Margolis, B. L., & Kroes, W. H. (1974) Work and the health of man. In: J. O'Toole (ed) Work and the Quality of Life. MIT Press, Cambridge, Mass.

Margolis, B. L., Kroes, W. H., & Quinn, R. P. (1974) Job stress; an unlisted occupational hazard. Journal of Occupational Medicine, 16, 652-661.

Marmot, M. G., & Madge, N. (1987) An epidemiological perspective on stress and health. In: S.V. Kasl & CL Cooper (eds) Stress and Health: Issues in Research Methodology, Wiley & Sons, Chichester.

Marmot, M. and Theorell, T. (1988) Social class and cardiovascular disease. The contribution of work. International Journal of Health Services, 18, 659-674.

Marshall, J. (1977) Job pressures and satisfactions at managerial levels. Unpublished PhD thesis, University of Manchester Institute of Science and Technology, Manchester.

Martin, R., & Wall, T. (1989) Attentional demand and cost responsibility as stressors in shop-floor jobs. Academy of Management Journal, 32, 69-86.

Martinez JMAG, & Martos MPB (1999) The meaning of work in persons with type-A behavior pattern. Psicothema, Vol.11, No.2, pp.357-366

Mason, J. W. (1968) A review of psychoendocrine research on the pituitary-adrenal cortical system. Psychosomatic Medicine, 30, 576-607.

Mason, J. W. (1971) A re-evaluation of the concept of non-specificity in stress theory. Journal of Psychiatric research, 8, 323.

Matteson, M.T., & Ivancevich, J.M. (1987) Controlling Work Stress. Jossey-Bass, San Fransisco.

Matthews, K. A., Glass, D. C., Rosenman, R. H., & Bortner, R. W. (1977) Competitive drive, pattern A and coronary heart disease: a further analysis of some data from the Western Collaborative Group Study. Journal of Chronic Diseases, 30, 489-498.

Meichenbaum, D. (1977) Cognitive-Behaviour Modification. Plenum Press, New York.

Meichenbaum, D. (1983) Coping with Stress. Century Publishing, London.

Meijman, T.F., Van Dormolen, M., Herber, R.F.M., Rongen, H. & Kuiper, S. (1995) Job stress, neuroendocrine activation, and immune status. In SL Sauter & LR Murphy (Eds.) Organizational risk factors for job stress. Washington, DC: APA.

Melamed S., Yekutieli D., Froom P., Kristal-Boneh E., Ribak J. (1999) Adverse work and environmental conditions predict occupational injuries - The Israeli Cardiovascular Occupational Risk Factors Determination in Israel (CORDIS) study. American Journal Of Epidemiology, Vol.150, No.1, pp.18-26

Milgram, N.A. (1982) War-related stress in Israeli children and youth. In L. Goldberger & S.Breznitz (eds) Handbook of Stress: Theoretical and Clinical Aspects. Free Press, New York.

Millar, D.J. (1984) The NIOSH suggested list of the ten leading work-related diseases and injuries. Journal of Occupational Medicine, 26, 340-341.

Millar, D.J. (1990) Mental health and workplace: interchangeable partnership. American Psychologist, 45, 1165-1166.

Miller, D.G., Grossman, Z.D., Richardson, R.L., Wistow, B.W., & Thomas, F.D. (1978) Effect of signalled versus unsignalled stress

on rat myocardium. Psychosomatic Medicine, 40, 432-434.

Miller, J. D. (1974) Effects of noise on people. Journal of the Acoustical Society of America, 56, 72-764.

Miller, S. (1979). Controllability and human stress: method, evidence and theory. Behavioural Research and Therapy, 17, 28-304.

Miller, S., Brody, D., & Summerton, J. (1988). Styles of coping with threat: implications for health. Journal of Personality and Social Psychology, 54, 142-148.

Ministry of Labour (1987) Survey on State of Employees' Health. Ministry of Labour, Tokyo, Japan.

Monjan, A.A. (1981) Stress and immunologic competence: studies in animals. In R. Ader (ed) Psychoneuroimmunology. Academic Press, New York.

Monk, T. H., & Tepas, D. (1985) Shift Work. In: CL Cooper & M. J. Smith (eds) Job Stress and Blue Collar Work. Wiley & Sons, Chichester.

Mudrack P.E. (1999) Time structure and purpose, Type A behavior, and the Protestant work ethic. Journal Of Organizational Behavior, Vol.20, No.2, pp.145- 158

Murphy, L.R. (1984) Occupational stress management: a review and appraisal. Journal of Occupational Psychology, 57, 1-15.

Murphy, L.R. (1988) Workplace interventions for stress reduction and prevention. In CL Cooper & R. Payne (Eds) Causes,

Coping and Consequences of Stress at Work.

Murphy, L.R., & Hurrell, J.J. (1987) Stress management in the process of occupational stress reduction. Journal of Managerial Psychology, 2, 18-23.

Murphy, L.R., Hurrell, J.J. & Quick, J.C. (1992) Work and well-being: where do we go from here? In J.C. Quick, L.R. Murphy, & J.J. Hurrell (eds) Stress and Well-being at Work: Assessments and Interventions for Occupational Mental Health. American Psychological Association, Washington DC.

Naitoh, P., Englund, C. E., & Ryman, D. H. (1983) Extending Human effectiveness During Sustained Operations Through Sleep Management. US Naval Health Research Center, San Diego, California.

Narayanan, V. K., & Nath, R. (1982) A field test of some attitudinal and behavioural consequences of flexitime. Journal of Applied Psychology, 67, 214-218.

National Institute of Occupational Safety and Health [NIOSH] (1988) Psychosocial Occupational Health. National Institute of Occupational Safety and Health, Washington, DC.

Neale, M.S., Singer, J., Schwartz, G.E., & Schwartz, J. (1983) Conflicting perspectives on stress reduction in occupational settings: a systems approach to their resolution. Report to NIOSH on P.O. No. 82-1058, Cincinnati, Ohio.

Neary, J., Elliott, K.V., & Toohey, J. (1992) The causes of workplace stress and strategies for management. Paper presented at the International Symposium on Work-related Diseases: Prevention and Health Promotion, Linz, Austria.

Nerell, G. (1975) Medical complaints and findings in Swedish sawmill workers. In: B. Thunell & B. Ager (eds) Ergonomics in Sawmill and Woodworking Industries. National Board of Occupational Safety and Health, Stockholm.

Neufeld, R. W. J., & Paterson, R. J. (1989) Issues concerning control and its implementation. In: R. W. J. Neufeld (ed) Advances in the Investigation of Psychological Stress. Wiley & Sons, New York.

Newman, J. E., & Beehr, T. A. (1979) Personal and organizational strategies for handling job stress: a review of research and opinion. Personnel Psychology, 32, 1-43.

Nobile, R.J. (1991) Matters of confidentiality. Personnel, 68, 11-12.

Nordhus, I.H., & Fleime, A.M. (1991) Job stress in two different care-giving contexts: a study of professional and semi-professional health personnel in Norway. Work & Stress, 5, 229-240.

Nowack, K.M. (1991) Psychological predictors of health status. Work & Stress, 5, 117-131.

Nutt, P. C. (1981) Evaluation Concepts and Methods: Shaping Policy for the Health Administrator. SP Medical and Scientific Books, New York.

O'Brien, G. E. (1982) The relative contribution of perceived skill-utilization and other perceived job attributes to the prediction of job satisfaction: cross validation study. Human Relations, 35, 219-237.

O'Hanlon, J. F. (1981) Boredom: practical consequences and a theory. Acta Psychologia, 49, 53-82.

O'Leary, A. (1990) Stress, emotion, and human immune function. Psychological Bulletin, 108, 363-382.

Organization for Economic Cooperation and Development [OECD] (1997) Joint Project on the Harmonization of Chemical Hazard/Risk Assessment Terminology. Internet WWW page at: http://www.who.ch/programmes/pcs/rsk_term/cvr_ltr.htm

Orpen, C. (1981) Effect of flexible working hours on employee satisfaction and performance. Journal of Applied Psychology, 66, 113-115.

Paffenbarger, R.S., Hale, W.E., Brand, R.J., & Hyde, R.T. (1977) Work-energy level, personal characteristics and fatal heart attack: a birth cohort effect. American Journal of Epidemiology, 105, 200-213.

Paffenbarger, R.S., Hyde, R.T., Wing, A.L., & Steinmetz, C.H. (1984) A natural history of athleticism and cardiovascular health. Journal of the American Medical Association, 252, 491-495.

Pahl, J. M., & Pahl, R. E. (1971) Managers and Their Wives. Allen Lane, London.

Parker, S.K., Chmiel, N. & Wall, T.D. (1997) Work characteristics and employee well-being within a context of strategic downsizing. Journal of Occupational health Psychology, 2(4) 289-303.

Patton, J. F., Vogel J. A., Damokosh, A. I., & Mello, R. P. (1989) Effects of continuous military operations on physical fitness capacity and physical performance. Work & Stress, 3, 69-77.

Payne, R. (1988) Individual differences in the study of occupational stress. In: CL Cooper & R. Payne (eds) Causes, Coping and Consequences of Stress at Work. Wiley & Sons, Chichester.

Payne, R., & Fletcher, B. (1983) Job demands, supports and constraints as predictors of psychological strain among school teachers. Journal of Vocational Behaviour, 22, 136-147.

Payne, R., & Hartley, J. (1987) A test of a model for exlaining the affective experience of unemployed men. Journal of Occupational Psychology, 60, 31-47.

Pearlin, L., & Schooler, C. (1978). The structure of coping. Journal of Health and Social Behavior, 19, 2-21.

Pearlin, L., Lieberman, M. L., Menaghan, E., & Mullan, J. T. (1981) The stress process. Journal of Health and Social Behaviour, 19, 2 - 21.

Pearse, R. (1977) What Managers Think About Their Managerial Careers. AMACOM, New York.

Perez A.D., Meizoso M.T.G., Gonzalez R.D. (1999) Validity of the structured interview for the assessment of Type A behavior pattern. European Journal Of Psychological Assessment, Vol.15, No.1, pp.39-48

Perkins, D. V. (1988) The assessment of stress using life events scales. In: L. Goldberg & S. Breznitz (eds) Handbook of Stress: Theoretical and Clinical Aspects. Free Press, New York.

Perrewe, P., & Ganster, D. C. (1989) The impact of job demands and behaviural control on experienced job stress. Journal of Organizational Behaviour, 10, 136-147.

ers M.L., Godaert G.L.R., Ballieux R.E., osschot J.F., Sweep F.C.G.J., Swinkels .M.J.W., vanVliet M., & Heijnen C.J. (1999) Immune responses to experimental stress: Effects of mental effort and uncontrollability Psychosomatic Medicine, Vol.61, No.4, pp.513-524

Peterson, P. (1981) Comparison of relaxation training, cognitive restructuring/behavioural training and multimodal stress management training seminars in an occupational setting. Dissertation submitted to Fuller Theological Seminary, Los Angeles, California.

Pierce, J.L. & Newstrom, J.W. (1983) The design of flexible work schedules and employee responses: relationships and processes. Journal of Occupational Behaviour, 4, 247-262.

Pollard T.M. (1997) Physiological consequences of everyday psychosocial stress Collegium Antropologicum, Vol.21, No.1, pp.17-28

Poppius E., Tenkanen L., Kalimo R., Heinsalmi P. (1999) The sense of coherence, occupation and the risk of coronary heart disease in the Helsinki Heart Study Social Science & Medicine, Vol.49, No.1, pp.109-120

Porter, L. W. (1990) Commitment patterns in industrial organizations. Paper to: Society for Industrial and Organizational psychology, Miami Beach, Florida (April).

Powell, L. H. (1987) Issues in the measurement of the Type A behaviour pattern. In: S. V. Kasl, & C.L. Cooper (eds) Stress and Health: Issues in Research Methodology. Wiley & Sons, Chichester.

Quick, J.C., & Quick, J.D. (1984) Organizational Stress and Preventive Management. McGraw-Hill, New York.

Quick, J.C., Murphy, L.R., & Hurrell, J.J. (1992a) Stress and Well-being at Work: Assessments and Interventions for Occupational Mental Health. American Psychological Association, Washington DC.

Quick, J.C., Joplin, J.R., Gray, D.A., & Cooley, E.C. (1993) The occupational life cycle and the family. In L.L'Abate (ed.), Handbook of Developmental Family Psychology and Psychopathology. Wiley & Sons, New York.

Quick, J. C., Murphy, L. R., Hurrell, J. J., & Orman, D. (1992b) The value of work, the risk of distress, and the power of prevention. In: J.C. Quick, L.R. Murphy, & J.J. Hurrell (eds) Stress & Well Being at Work: Assessments and Interventions for Occupational Mental Health. American Psychological Association, Washington DC.

Quick, J.C., Camara, W.J., Hurrell, J.J., Johnson, J.V., Piotrkowski, C.S., Sauter, S.L., & Spielberger, C.D. (1997) Introduction and historical overview. Journal of Occupational Health Psychology, 2 (1), 3-6

Rahe, R. H. (1969) Multi-cultural correlations of life change scaling: America, Japan, Denmark, and Sweden. Journal of Psychosomatic Research, 13, 191-195.

Repetti, R. L. (1987) Linkages between work and family roles. In: S. Oskamp (ed) Applied Social Psychology Annual Vol 7. Family Processes and Problems. Sage, Beverly Hills.

Repetti, R. L., & Crosby, F. (1984) Gender and depression: exploring the adult role explanation. Journal of Social and Clinical Psychology, 2, 57-70.

Repetti, R. L., Matthews, R. A., & Waldron, I. (1989) Employment and women's health: effects of paid employment on women's mental and physical health. American Psychologist, 44, 1394-1401.

Rice, H.K. (1963) The responding-rest ratio in the production of gastric ulcers in the rat. Psychological Reports, 13, 11-14.

Richter, P., & Schmidt, C. F. (1988) Arbeitsanforderungen und Beanspruchungsbewältigung bei Herzinfarkt-Patienten - ein tätigkeitspsychologischer Diagnostikansatz. In: H. Schröder & J. Guthke (Hrsg.) Fortschritte der klinischen Persönlichkeitspsychologie und klinischen Psychodiagnostik. Barth, Leipzig. pp 49-56 (Psychotherapie und Grenzgebiete, 9).

Richter, P., Rudolph, M., & Schmidt, C. F. (1995) FABA: Fragebogen zur Analyse belastungsrelevanter Anforderungsbewältigung. Technische Universität, Institut für Arbeits-, Organisations- und Sozialpsychologie, Dresden (Methodensammlung, 4).

Riley, V. (1979) Stress - cancer contradictions: a continuing puzzlement. Cancer Detection and Prevention, 2, 159-162

Riley, V. (1981) Psychoneuroendocr fluences on immunocompetence ar plasia. Science, 212, 1100-1109.

Riley, V., Fitzmaurice, M. A., & Sp D. H. (1981) Psychoneuroimmur factors in neoplasia: studies in an R. Ader (ed) Psychoneuroimmι Academic Press, New York.

Rimon, R.A. & Laakso, R. (1985) Lif and rheumatoid arthritis: a 15-year t up study. Psychotherapy and Psychι matics, 43, 38-43.

Robertson, I. T., & Cooper, CL (1983) Hι man Behaviour in Organizations. MacDc ald and Evans Ltd., London.

Ronen, S. (1981) Flexible Working Hours; An Innovation in the Quality of Work Life. McGraw Hill, New York.

Rosa, R.R. & Colligan, M.J. (1986) The NIOSH Fatigue Test Battery: Laboratory Validation of a Portable System for Field Study of Extended Workdays and Work Scheduling. NIOSH internal report. National Institute for Occupational Health, Cincinnati.

Rosa, R. R., Colligan, M. J., & Lewis, P. (1989) Extended workdays: effects of 8-hour and 12-hour rotating shifts schedules on performance, subjective aleartness, sleep patterns and psychosocial variables. Work & Stress, 3, 2-32.

Rose, R. M., Poe, R. O., & Mason, J. W. (1967) Observations on the relationship between psychological state, 17-OHCS excretion and epinephrine, norepinephrine, insulin, BEI, estrogen and androgen levels during basic training. Psychosomatic Medicine, 29, 544.

enman, R. H., Friedman, M., Straus, R., m, M., Kositchek, R., Hahn, W., & thessen, N. T. (1964a) A predictive y of coronary heart disease: appendix. nal of the American Medical Association, 189, 1-4.

senman, R. H., Friedman, M., Straus, R., /urm, M., Kositchek, R., Hahn, W., & Werthessen, N. T. (1964b) A predictive study of coronary heart disease. Journal of the American Medical Association, 189, 113-124.

Rosenstock, L. (1997) Work organization research at the National Institute for Occupational Safety and Health. Journal of Occupational Health Psychology, 2(1), 7-100

Rotheiler, E., Richter, P. Rudolf, M. & Hinton, J. W. (1997) Further cross-cultural factor validation on the FABA self report inventory of coronary-prone behaviours. Psychology and Health 12, 505-512.

Russek, H. I., & Zohman, B. L. (1958) Relative significance of heredity, diet and occupational stress in CHD of young adults. American Journal of Medical Sciences, 235, 266-275.

Rutenfranz, J. (1982) Occupational health measures for night and shift workers. Journal of Human Ergology, 11 (supplement), 67-86.

Rutenfranz, J., Haider, M., & Koller, M. (1985) Occupational health measures for night workers and shift workers. In: S. Folkard & T. H. Monk (eds) Hours of Work: Temporal Factors in Work Scheduling. Wiley & Sons, Chichester.

Rutenfranz, J., Colquhoun, W. P., Knauth, P., & Ghata, J. N. (1977) Biomedical and psychosocial aspects of shift work: a review. Scandinavian Journal of Work and Environmental Health, 3, 165-182.

Ryman, D.H., & Ursin, H. (1979) Factor analyses of the physiological responses of company commanders to stress. Quoted in : Ursin, H. (1979) Personality, activation and somatic health: a new psychosomatic theory. In: S. Levine & H. Ursin (eds) Coping and Health. Plenum Press, New York.

Ryman, D.H., Naitoh, P., & Englund, C. E. (1989) Perceived exertion under conditions of sustained work and sleep loss. Work & Stress, 3, 5-68.

Salo, K. (1995) Teacher stress and coping over an autumn term in Finland. Work & Stress, 9 (1), 55-66.

Salvendy, G., & Smith, M. (1981) Machine Pacing and Occupational Stress. Wiley & Sons, Chichester.

Sandler, I N., And Lakey, B. (1982). Locus of control as stress moderator: the role of control perceptions and social support. American Journal of Community Psychology, 10, 65-79

Sarason, I. G., de Monchaux, C., & Hunt, T. (1975) Methodological issues in the assessment of life stress. In: L. Levi (ed) Emotions: Their Parameters and Measurement. Raven, New York.

Saunders, D. (1956). Moderator variables in prediction.Educational and Psychological Measurement, 16, 209-222.

Sauter, S. L. (1992) Introduction to the NIOSH proposed National Strategy. In: G.P. Keita & S.L. Sauter (eds) Work and Well Being: An Agenda for the 1990s. American Psychological Association, Washington DC.

Sauter, S.L. & Murphy, L.R. (1995) Organizational risk factors for job stress. Washington, DC: APA

Sauter, S.L., Hurrell, J.J., & Cooper, CL (1989) Job Control and Worker Health. Wiley & sons, Chichester.

Sauter, S. L., Murphy, L.R., & Hurrell, J.J. (1990) Prevention of work-related psychological disorders: A national strategy proposed by the National Insitute for Occupational Safety and Health (NIOSH). American Psychologist, 45, 146-158.

Sauter, S. L., Murphy, L. R., & Hurrell, J. J. (1992) Prevention of work related psychological disorders: a national strategy proposed by the National Institute for Occupational Safety and Health. In: G. P. Keita & S. L. Sauter (eds) Work and Well-Being: An Agenda for the 1990s. American Psychological Association, Washington DC.

Sauter, S.L., Hurrell, J. J., Jr., Murphy, L.R., & Levi, L. (Eds.). (1998). Psychosocial and organizational factors. In J.M. Stellman (Ed.) Encyclopaedia of Occupational

Health and Safety, Fourth Edition, 2, pp. 34.2-34.6. Geneva, Switzerland: International Labour Organization

Schaubroeck, J. & Merritt, D.E. (1997) Divergent effects of job control on coping with work stressors:The key role of self-efficacy. Academy Of Management Journal, 40, 738-754

Scheck,C.L., Kinicki,A.J., Davy, J.A. (1997) Testing the mediating processes between work stressors and subjective well-being. Journal Of Vocational Behavior, 50, 96-123

Scheuch, K. (1990): Psychosoziale Faktoren im Arbeitsprozeß und Gesundheit: Einführung. Z. ges. Hyg. 36, 403-407

Scheuch, K. (1996): Stress and resources at work in a changing society. Bremerhaven: Wirtschaftsverlag NW, pp.95-109 (Schriftenreihe der Bundesanstalt für Arbeitsmedizin: Tagungsbericht 11)

Schneiderman, N. (1978) Animal models relating behavioural stress and cardiovascular pathology. In T. Dembroski (ed) Proceedings of the Forum on Coronary-Prone Behaviour. DHEW publication no.(NIH) 78-1451. US Government Printing Office, Washington DC.

Schonpflug, F. & Battmann, A. (1988) The costs and benefits of coping. In: S. Fisher & J. Reason (eds) Handbook of Life Stress, Cognition and Health. Wiley & Son, Chichester

Schott, F. (1992) Panel comments: work design. In: G. P. Keita & S. L. Sauter (eds) Work and Well-Being: An Agenda for the

1990s. American Psychological Association, Washington DC.

Schriber, J.B. & Gutek, B.A. (1987) Some time dimensions of work: measurement of an underlying aspect of organizational culture. Journal of Applied Psychology, 7, 624-650.

Schrijvers C.T.M., van de Mheen H.D., Stronks K, Mackenbach JP (1998) Socioeconomic inequalities in health in the working population: the contribution of working conditions. International Journal Of Epidemiology, Vol.27, No.6, pp.1011-1018

Schwartz, G. (1980) Stress management in occupational settings. Public Health Reports, 95, 99-108.

Scott, R., & Howard, A. (1970) Models of stress. In: S. Levine & N. Scotch (eds) Social Stress. Aldine, Chicago.

Scriven, M. (1967) The methodology of evaluation. In: R. E. Stake (ed) Perspectives of Curriculum Evaluation. AERA Monograph Series on Curriculum Evaluation no. 1, Rand McNally, Chicago.

Sells, S. B. (1970) On the nature of stress. In: J. McGrath (ed) Social and Psychological factors in Stress. Holt, Rinehart & Winston, New York.

Selye, H. (1936) A syndrome produced by diverse nocuous agents. Nature, 138, 32.

Selye, H. (1950) Stress, Acta Incorporated, Montreal.

Selye, H. (1956) Stress of Life. McGraw-Hill, New York.

Selye, H. (1976) Stress in Health and Disease. Butterworths, Boston.

Sharit, J., & Salvendy, G. (1982) Occupational stress: review and appraisal. Human Factors, 24, 129-162.

Sheffield, D., Dobbie, D. & Carroll, D. (1994) Stress, social support, and psychological wellbeing in secondary school teachers. Work & Stress, 8 (3), 235-243.

Shekelle, R. B., Ostfeld, A. M., & Paul, O. (1969) Social status and incidence of CHD. Journal of Chronic Disorders, 22, 381-394.

Shekelle, R. B., Gale, M., Ostfeld, A. M., & Paul, O. (1983) Hostility, risk of coronary heart disease, and mortality. Psychosomatic Medicine, 45, 109-114.

Shilling, S., & Brackbill, R.M. (1987) Occupational health and safety risks and potential health consequences perceived by US workers. Public Health Reports, 102, 36-46.

Shinn, M, Rosario, M, Morch, H & Chestnut, D.E. (1984) Coping with job stress and burnout in the human services. Journal of Personality and Social Psychology, 46, 864-876.

Shirom, A., Eden, D., Silberwasser, S., & Kellerman, J. J. (1973) Job stresses and risk factors in CHD among occupational categories in kibbutzim. Social Science and Medicine, 7, 875-892.

Siegrist, J. (1990) Chronischer Distress und koronares Risiko: Neue Erkenntnisse und ihre Bedeutung für die Pravention. In: M. Arnold, C. v. Ferber, & K.-D. Henke (Hrsg.)

Ökonomie der Prävention. Bleicher, Gerlingen.

Sigman, A. (1992) The state of corporate health care. Personnel Management, 47-61.

Simon R.I. (1999) Chronic posttraumatic stress disorder: A review and checklist of factors influencing prognosis. Harvard Review Of Psychiatry, Vol.6, No.6, pp.304-312

Singer, J.A., Neale, M.S., Schwartz, G.E., & Schwartz, J. (1986) Conflicting perspectives on stress reduction in occupational settings: a systems approach to their resolution. In M.F. Cataldo & T.J. Coates (eds) Health and Industry: A Behavioural Medicine Perspective. Wiley & Sons, New York.

Sklar, L. S., & Anisman, H. (1981) Stress and cancer. Psychological Bulletin, 89, 36-406.

Sleeper, R. D. (1975) Labour mobility over the life cycle. British Journal of Industrial Relations, 13.

Smewing, C., and Cox, T. (1996) The organizational health of health care institutions in the United Kingdom. Proceedings of the IV Seminar on Organizational Psychology of Health Care, European Network of Organizational Psychologists, Munich.

Smith, A. (1991) A review of the non auditory effects of noise on health. Work & Stress, 5, 49-62.

Smith, M.J. (1985) Machine-paced work and stress. In CL Cooper & M.J. Smith (eds) Job Stress and Blue Collar Work. Wiley & sons, Chichester.

Smith, M.J., Hurrell, J.J., & Murphy, R.K. (1981) Stress and health effects in paced and unpaced work. In G. Salvendy & M.J. Smith (eds) Pacing and Occupational Stress. Taylor and Francis, London.

Smith, R. P. (1981) Boredom: a review. Human factors, 23, 329-340.

Spector, P. E. (1986) Perceived control by employees: a meta analysis of studies concerning autonomy and participation in decision making. Human Relations, 39, 1005-1016.

Spector, P.E. (1987a) Interactive effects of perceived control and job stressors on affective reactions and health outcomes for clerical workers. Work & Stress, 1, 155-162.

Spector, P.E. (1987b) Method variance as an artifact in self-reported affect and perceptions at work: Myth or significant problem? Journal of Applied Psychology, 72 (3), 438-443.

Spielberger, C.D. (1976) The nature and measurement of anxiety. In C.D. Spielberger and R. Diaz-Guerrero (eds) Cross-Cultural Anxiety. Hemisphere, Washington DC.

Spurgeon, A., & Harrington, J. M. (1989) Work performance and health of junior hospital doctors - a review of the literature. Work & Stress, 3, 117-128.

Spurgeon A., Harrington J.M., & Cooper C.L. (1997) Health and safety problems associated with long working hours: A review of the current position. Occupational And Environmental Medicine, Vol.54, No.6, pp.367-375

Stainbrook, G. L., & Green, L. W. (1983) Role of psychosocial stress in cardiovascular disease. Houston Heart Bulletin, 3, 1-8.

Stampi, C. (1989) Polyphasic sleep strategies improve prolonged sustained performance: a field study on 99 sailors. Work & Stress, 3, 41-55.

Standing, H. & Nicolini, D. (1997) Review of Work-Related Violence. Health & Safety Executive Contract Research Report 143/1997. Sudbury, Suffolk, U.K.: HSE Books.

Stansfeld, S.A., Fuhrer, R., Shipley, M.J. & Marmot, M.G. (1999) Work characteristics predict psychiatric disorder: prospective results from the Whitehall II study. Occupational and Environmental Medicine, 56, 302-307

Stansfeld, S.A., North, F.M., White, I. & Marmot, M.G. (1995) Work characteristics and psychiatric disorder in civil servants in London. Journal of epidemiology and Community Health, 49, 48-53.

Stein, M., Keller, S., & Schleifer, S. (1981) The hypothalamus and the immune response. In H. Weiner, M. Hofer, & A. Stunkard (eds) Brain, Behaviour and Bodily Disease. Raven, New York.

Stewart, R. (1976) Contrasts in Management. McGraw-Hill, New York.

Stone, E.A. (1975) Stress and catecholamines. In A. Friedhoff (ed) Catecholamiones and Behaviour, Vol 2. Plenum, New York.

Strauss, G. (1974) Workers: attitudes and adjustments. In the American Assesmbly,

Columbia University, The Worker and the Job: Coping with Change. Prentice-Hall, Englewood Cliffs, NJ.

Surtees P.G. & Wainwright N.W.J (1998) Adversity over the life course: assessment and quantification issues. Stress Medicine, vol. 14, no. 4, pp. 205-211

Susser, M. (1967) Causes of peptic ulcer: a selective epidemiological review. Journal of Chronic Diseases, 20, 435-456.

Sutherland, V. J., & Cooper, CL (1990) Understanding stress: psychological persepctive for health professionals. Psychology & Health, series: 5. Chapman and Hall, London.

Symonds, C.P. (1947) Use and abuse of the term flying stress. In Air Ministry, Psychological Disorders in Flying Personnel of the Royal Air Force, Investigated during the War, 1939-1945. HMSO, London.

Szabo, S., Maull, E.A., & Pirie, J. (1983) Occupational Stress: understanding, recognition and prevention. Experientia, 39, 1057-1180.

Tavistock Institute of Human Relations (1986) Violence to Staff: A Basis for Assessment and Prevention. HMSO, London.

Terry, D.J. & Jimmieson, N.L (1999) Work control and employee well-being: A decade review. In Cooper & Robertson (Eds) International review of industrial and organizational psychology 1999, Vol. 14. (pp. 95-148). Chichester, England UK: American Ethnological Press.

Theorell, T. (1997) Fighting for and losing or gaining control in life. Acta Physiologica Scandinavica, 161, Suppl. 640, 107-111.

Thompson, S.C. (1981) Will it hurt less if I can control it? A complex answer to a simple question. Psychological Bulletin, 90, 89-101.

Thomson, L., Griffiths, A., Cox, T. (1998) The psychometric quality of self-reported absence data. Proceedings of the International Work Psychology Conference. University of Sheffield, Institute of Work Psychology. ISBN 0 9533504 0 1.

Turkkan, J.S., Brady, J.V., & Harris A.H. (1982) Animal studies of stressful interactions: a behavioural-physiological overview. In L. Goldberger & S. Breznitz (eds) Handbook of Stress: Theoretical and Clinical Aspects. Free Press, New York.

Turnage, J. J., & Spielberger, C.D. (1991) Job stress in managers, professionals and clerical workers. Work & Stress, 5, 165-176.

Ulrich, R.E., & Azrin, N.H. (1962) Reflexive fighting in response to aversive stimulation. Journal of the Experimental Analysis of Behaviour, 5, 511-520.

Uris, A. (1972) How managers ease job pressures. International Management, June, 45-46.

Ursin, H. (1979) Personality, activation and somatic health: a new psychosomatic theory. In: S. Levine & H. Ursin (eds) Coping and Health. Plenum Press, New York.

Ursin, H., Mykletun, R., Tonder, O., Vaernes, R. J., Relling, G., Isaksen, E., &

Murisaon, R. (1984) Psychological stress factors and concentrations of immunoglobulins and complement components in humans. Scandinavian Journal of Psychology, 23, 193-199.

United States Department of Health and Human Services USDHHS (1980) New Developments in Occupational Stress: Proceedings of a Conference. US Department of Health and Human Services, no: NIOSH 81-102, US Government Printing Office, Washington DC.

Vaernes, R. J., Warncke, M., Eidsvik, S., Aakvaag, A., Tonder, O., & Ursin, H. (1987) Relationships between perceived health and psychological factors among submarine personnel: endocrine and immunological effects. In: A. Marroni & G. Oriani (eds) Diving and Hyperbaric Medicine. Academic Press, New York.

Vaernes, R. J., Myhre, G., Aas, H., Homnes, T., Hansen, I., & Tonder, O. (1991) Relationships between stress, psychological factors, health and immune levels among military aviators. Work & Stress, 5, 5-16.

Vaernes, R. J., Knardahl, S., Romsing, J., Aakvaag, A., Tonder, O., Walter, B., & Ursin, H. (1988) Relationships between environmental problems, defense strategies and health among shiftworkers in the process industry. Work & Stress, 1, 7-15.

Van der Hek, H. & Plomp, H.N. (1997) Occupational stress management programmes: a practical overview of published effect studies. Occupational Medicine, 47 (3), 133-141.

Van Raaij, M.T.M., Oortgiesen, M., Tim-
merman, H.H., Dobbe, C.J.G., & VanLov-
eren, H. (1996) Time-dependent
differential changes of immune function in
rats exposed to chronic intermittent noise.
Physiology & Behavior, Vol.60, No.6,
pp.1527-1533

Viswesvaran C., Sanchez J.I. & Fisher J.
(1999) The role of social support in the
process of work stress: A meta-analysis.
Journal Of Vocational Behavior, Vol.54,
No.2, pp.314-334

Volhardt, B.R., Ackerman, S.H., Grayzel,
A.I., & Barland, P. (1982) Psychologicaly
distinguishable groups of rheumatoid
arthritis patients: a controlled single blind
study. Psychosomatic Medicine, 44, 353-
361.

Von Restorff, W., Kleinhanss, G., Schaad,
G., & Gorges, W. (1989) Combined work
stresses: effect of reduced air renewal on
psychological performance during 72hr
sustained operations. Work & Stress, 3,
15-20.

Voydanoff, P., & Kelly, R. F. (1984) Determinants of work-related family problems
among employed parents. Journal of Marriage and the Family, 46, 881-892.

Wall, T.D. & Clegg, C.W. (1981) A longitudinal study of group work redesign. Journal of Occupational Behaviour, 2, 31-49.

Wallhagen M.I., Strawbridge W.J., Cohen
R.D., Kaplan G.A. (1997) An increasing
prevalence of hearing impairment and associated risk factors over three decades of
the Alameda County Study. American

Journal Of Public Health, Vol.87, No.3,
pp.440- 442

Wardell, W. I., Hyman, M., & Bahnson, C B.
(1964) Stress and coronary heart disease in
three field studies. Journal of Chronic Diseases, 17, 73-84.

Warr, P. B. (1982) Psychological aspects of
employment and unemployment. Psychological Medicine, 12, 7-11.

Warr, P. B. (1983) Work, jobs and unemployment. Bulletin of the British Psychological Society, 36, 305-311.

Warr, P. B. (1987) Work, Unemployment
and Mental Health. Cambridge University
Press, Cambridge.

Warr, P. B. (1990) Decision latitude, job demands and employee well-being. Work &
Stress, 4, 285-294.

Warr, P. B. (1992) Job features and exces-
sive stress. In: R. Jenkins & N. Coney (eds)
Prevention of Mental Ill Health at Work.
HMSO, London.

Warshaw, L.J. (1979) Managing Stress. Ad-
dison-Wesley, Reading, Mass.

Waterhouse, J.M., Folkhard, S., & Minors ,
D.S. (1992) Shiftwork, Health and Safety:
An Overview of the Scientific Literature
1978-1990. HMSO, London.

Watson, D. & Clark, L.A. (1984) Negative
affectivity: The disposition to experience
aversive emotional states. Psychological
Bulletin, 96 (3), 465-490.

Webb, E. J., Campbell, D. T., Schwartz, R.
D. & Sechrest, L. (1966) Unobtrusive Mea-

sures: Nonreactive Research in the Social Sciences. Rand McNally, Chicago.

Weinberg A., Cooper C.L., & Weinberg A. (1999) Workload, stress and family life in British Members of Parliament and the psychological impact of reforms to their working hours. Stress Medicine, Vol.15, No.2, pp.79-87

Weiner, H. (1977) Psychobiology and Human Disease. Elsevier, New York.

Weiss, J.M. (1972) Psychological factors in stress and disease. Scientific American, 226, 104-113.

Weitzman, E.D., Boyar, R.M., Kapen, S., & Hellman, L. (1975) The relationship of sleep and sleep stages to neuroendocrine secretion and biological rhythms in man. Recent Progress Hormone Research, 31, 399-446.

Welford, A. T. (1973) Stress and performance. Ergonomics, 16, 567-580.

Wheaton, B. (1983) Stress, personal coping resources and psychiatric symptoms: an investigation of interactive model. Journal of Health and Social behaviour, 24.

Wilensky, H. (1960) Work, careers and social integration. International Social Science Journal, 4, 54 -560.

Williams, R. B., Barefoot, J. C., & Shekelle, R. B. (1985) The health consequences of hostility. In: M. A. Chesney & R. H. Rosenman (eds) Anger and Hostility in Cardiovascular and behavioural Disorders. Hemisphere Publishing Corp., Washington DC.

Williams, R. B., Haney, T. L., Lee, K. L., Kong, Y., Blumenthal, J. A., & Whalen, R. E.(1980) Type A behaviour, hostility and coronary atherosclerosis. Psychosomatic Medicine, 42, 539-549.

Windel A, Zimolong B. (1997) Group work and performance in business. Gruppendynamik-Zeitschrift Fur Angewandte Sozialpsychologie, 28 (4), pp.333-35

Winnubst, J. A. M., & Schabracq, M. J. (1996) Social Support, Stress and Organization: Towards Optimal Matching. In : M. J. Schabracq, J. A. M. Winnubst, & C. L. Cooper (eds) Handbook of work and health psychology. John Wiley & Sons, Chichester.

World Health Organization [WHO] (1986) Constitution of the World Health Organization. In: Basic Documents (36th ed). World Health Organization, Geneva.

Wykes, J. & Whittington, R. (1991) Coping strategies used by staff following assault by a patient: an exploratory study. Work & Stress, 5 (1), 37-48.

Wyler, A., Masuda, M., & Holmes, T. (1968) Seriousness of illness scale. Journal of Psychosomatic Research, 11, 363-375.

Wynne, R., Clarkin, N., Cox, T., & Griffiths, A. (1997). Guidance on the Prevention of Violence at Work. Luxembourg: European Commission, DG-V.

Zegans, L.S. (1982) Stress and the Development of Somatic Disorders. In L.Goldberger & S. Breznitz (eds) Handbook of Stress: Theoretical and Clinical Aspects. Free Press, New York.

APPENDIX 1. PROJECT ORGANISATION

Agency's Project Manager

Dr. M. Aaltonen
European Agency for Safety and Health at Work
Gran Via, 33
E-48009 Bilbao
SPAIN

Project Consultants

Prof. Tom Cox CBE
Dr. Amanda Griffiths
Mr. Eusebio Rial-González
Institute of Work, Health and Organisa-
'ions (I-WHO)
.iversity of Nottingham Business School
ottingham NG8 1BB
NITED KINGDOM

oject members within the Topic
ntre on Research - Work and Health

Dr. V. Borg (Task leader)
National Institute of Occupational Health -
Arbejdsmiljøinstituttet (AMI)

Lersoe Parkallé 105
DK-2100 COPENHAGEN
DENMARK

Dr. A. Brouwers
TNO Work and Employment (TNO)
P.O. Box 718
2130 AS HOOFDDORP
The NETHERLANDS

Dr. K. Kuhn
Bundesanstalt für Arbeitsschutz und Ar-
beitsmedizin (BAuA)
Friedrich-Henkel-Weg 1-25
D-44149 DORTMUND
GERMANY

Dr. M. Neboit
Dr. P. Méreau
Institut National de Recherche et de Sécu-
rité (INRS)
Centre de Recherche et de Formation
Avenue de Bourgogne, P.O. Box 27
54501 VANDOEUVRE CEDEX
FRANCE

Dra. S. Nogareda
Centro Nacional de Condiciones de Traba-
jo (INSHT)
c/Dulcet 2-10
08034 BARCELONA
SPAIN

Lead Organisation of the Topic Centre on Research - Work and Health

Dr. J-L. Marié
Dr. J-C. André
Institut National de Recherche et de Sécu-
rité (INRS)
30 rue Olivier Noyer
F-75014 PARIS
FRANCE